Once Upon a Knit

28 GRIMM AND GLAMOROUS FAIRY-TALE PROJECTS

Genevieve Miller

POTTER CRAFT

NEW YORK

Acknowledgments

This book would not be possible without several people and a few good fairies. Special thanks to my family and friends, especially my husband, Wayne, and my children, Sean, Grace, and Madeline. Their support, encouragement, and infinite patience with me during this process has been astounding. Thanks to Kate Epstein for being a champion of creativity. Thanks to Betty Wong, Caitlin Harpin, and the entire team at Potter Craft for turning ideas into reality and for their exceptional attention to detail. Thanks to all my fellow designers who worked magic on these amazing projects—your creativity never ceases to amaze me! A big thanks goes to Eve Ng and Amy Polcyn for tech editing patterns from so many designers. Special thanks to Therese Chynoweth for creating all the beautiful charts in the book. Thanks to Rebecca Little for taking my photo up at the Hollywood Bowl and to Amy Sly for the stunning visual design. Thanks to everyone who has cheered me on along the way. And a giant-size thanks to the following yarn companies that provided yarn support for *Once Upon a Knit*!

KnitPicks	Three Irish Girls	Habu Textiles
Skacel Collection, Inc.	Neighborhood Fiber	Tilli Tomas
Brown Sheep Yarn Company	Company	Madelinetosh

A portion of the proceeds of this book will be donated to the Make-A-Wish Foundation, who have been granting wishes to very ill children since 1981.

Copyright © 2014 by Mary Genevieve Miller
Photographs and illustrations copyright © 2014 by Potter Craft, an imprint of the Crown Publishing Group, a division of Random House LLC.

Published in the United States by Potter Craft, an imprint of the Crown Publishing Group, a division of Random House LLC, a Penguin Random House Company, New York.
www.pottercraft.com
www.crownpublishing.com

POTTER CRAFT and colophon are registered trademarks of Random House LLC.

Library of Congress Cataloging-in-Publication Data
Miller, Genevieve
  Once upon a knit : 28 Grimm and glamorous fairy-tale projects / Genevieve Miller. — first edition.
    p. cm

1. Knitting—Patterns. 2. Costume. 3. Fairy tales. I. Title.
  TT825.M563 2014
  746.43'2—dc23
                          2013011851

ISBN 978-0-385-34494-4
eBook ISBN 978-0-385-34495-1
Printed in China

Design by Amy Sly
Project photographs by Heather Weston
Photograph on page 144 by Rebecca Little
Cover design by Amy Sly
Cover photographs by Heather Weston

Standard Yarn Weight System chart on page 134 used with permission of the Craft Yarn Council of America (www.yarnstandards.com).

10 9 8 7 6 5 4 3 2 1
First Edition

Contents

INTRODUCTION 6

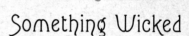

Introduction

nce upon a time there lived a little girl who loved stories. She believed in children who fell down rabbit holes, plucky girls who brought goodies to their grandmothers, and princesses who lived with dwarfs and fairies. Though she never talked to mermaids or spun straw into gold, she discovered her own magical gift: knitting beautiful garments with two sticks and a ball of yarn.

Though it's been a while since I was that little girl, I still believe in the magic of fairy tales—and knitting. And I've met many other fairy godmothers who believe, too. Some of us are disguised as moms, others as teachers, and two as roller-derby girls. My knitter friends and I, who honed our designing skills for *Vampire Knits,* have been absolutely entranced by modern grown-up versions of fairy tales. Ancient folktales inspired modern classics like the Broadway musical *Into the Woods* and the beloved animated tales from Disney that we grew up with. More recently, fairy tales have invaded pop culture on a grand scale, with blockbuster movies and television shows like *Once Upon a Time.* It's a good time to be a fan of fairy tales. In recent versions, Snow White is a strong, confident archer, Hansel and Gretel are witch hunters, and the evil sorceress from *Sleeping Beauty* is a sympathetic character. Meanwhile, the costumes in these revisionist tales have captivated us with their decadent embellishments, feminine silhouettes, and fantastical luxury.

The twenty-eight projects in *Once Upon a Knit* are destined to add a touch of romance and adventure to your everyday wardrobe. A beautiful lace shawl and dainty fingerless mitts can help anyone feel like a princess. And every brave warrior needs a pair of cozy socks or a warm sweater to remind him (or her) of home. In this book you'll find projects that remind you of fairy tales from your childhood and of not-quite-suitable-for-children shows that have turned those bedtime stories into twisted, yet beautiful, fantasies. You'll find grown-up garments inspired by both good and evil characters, cute costumes for children, charming accessories, and toys for all ages.

Why do fairy tales continue to lure us in? Simply put, they help us believe in ourselves. Fairy tales are full of hope—hope that great things can happen to ordinary people, or that a frog may become a prince if only a kindhearted person kisses him. Fairy tales teach us to be kind to one another, to beware of a jealousy that can devour your soul, and to fend off villains who darken our lives.

I hope that the designs in this book will inspire you to be the hero or heroine of your own fairy tale and that your happily ever after includes handknits you'll want to wear every day. Come with us into this wonderland. It's grim, but it's gorgeous.

Into the Woods

nce upon a time there was an enchanted forest, inhabited by magical creatures of all kinds. Fairies danced around tree stumps, trolls hid under bridges, and a family of bears kept a quaint little home. Princes and princesses rode on their steeds from one kingdom to the next, often encountering all sorts of trouble along the way (but more on that later). Should you find yourself lost in these woods, be careful whom you talk to, and never walk uninvited into strangers' houses.

In this chapter you'll find projects to protect travelers in the Enchanted Forest, such as Red Riding Hood's iconic accessories, a richly patterned scarf and matching gloves for rugged hunters, a blanket for chilly nights, socks for climbing beanstalks, and a magical bag that Dorothy Gale would envy. Customize a hat for your favorite little critter, or make a ballerina skirt and wand for a spritely fairy. Not too ordinary but not too outlandish either, these projects are just right for adding a touch of whimsy to your day.

Ruby Red Riding Hood

This cozy cloak is a grown-up version of the classic Little Red Riding Hood cape, but it can be sized to fit little girls just as well. The checkerboard border complements the gingham pattern of Little Red's Basket (page 14).

←— DESIGNED BY GENEVIEVE MILLER —→

SKILL LEVEL

Easy

SIZES

Child (Adult)

FINISHED MEASUREMENTS

Shoulder width: 62½ (76¾)" (159 [195]cm)

Length: 24 (32)" (61 [81]cm)

Hem width: 32 (36¾)" (81 [93]cm)

MATERIALS

✦ SimpliWorsted by HiKoo (55% superwash merino, 28% acrylic, 17% nylon; 1¾ oz/50g, 117 yd/107m): 9 (16) skeins in 016 Gypsy Red (4) MEDIUM

✦ Size 7 (4.5mm) 32" (80cm) circular needle, or size needed to obtain gauge

✦ Stitch markers

✦ Tapestry needle

✦ Matching thread and sewing needle

✦ 2 buttons, ¾" (2cm) in diameter

GAUGE

20 stitches and 28 rows = 4" (10cm) in stockinette stitch

SPECIAL SKILLS

3-needle bind-off (page 135)

Fairy Facts

Vampires, meet fairy tales. In both *Buffy the Vampire Slayer* and *True Blood*, characters dress as the iconic girl in the red cloak.

Cloak

Cast on 160 (184) stitches.

Row 1 (RS): K4, p4, k4, pm, *p4, k4; repeat from * to the last 12 stitches, pm, p4, k4, p4.

Rows 2–4: *K4, p4; repeat from * to end.

Rows 5–8: *P4, k4; repeat from * to end.

Rows 9 and 11: *K4, p4, k4, sm, kfb, knit to marker, kfb, sm, p4, k4, p4—2 stitches increased.

Rows 10 and 12: *K4, p4, k4, sm, purl to marker, sm, p4, k4, p4.

Rows 13 and 15: *P4, k4, p4, sm, kfb, knit to marker, kfb, sm, k4, p4, k4—2 stitches increased.

Rows 14 and 16: *P4, k4, p4, sm, purl to marker, sm, k4, p4, k4.

Repeat Rows 9–16 18 (24) more times, then Rows 9–12 once—316 (388) stitches.

Buttonhole Row 1: *P4, bind off 2 stitches, k2, p4, sm, kfb, knit to marker, kfb, sm, k4, p2, bind off 2 stitches, k4.

Buttonhole Row 2: *P4, cast on 2 stitches, k2, p4, sm, purl to marker, sm, k4, p2, cast on 2 stitches, k4.

Work Rows 1–16 of pattern—320 (392) stitches.

Decrease Row 1 (RS): K4, p4, *k2, k2tog; repeat from * to the last 8 stitches, k4, p4—244 (298) stitches.

Decrease Row 2: K4, p4, *p1, p2tog; repeat from * to the last 8 stitches, k4, p4—168 (204) stitches.

Next row: K4, p4, k4, bind off 144 (180) stitches snugly, p4, k4, p4.

Hood

Setup row (WS): K4, p4, k4, pick up and k70 (94) stitches purlwise evenly across the bound-off stitches, p4, k4, p4—94 (118) stitches.

Row 1: *P4, k4, p4, pm, knit to the last 12 stitches, pm, k4, p4, k4.

Row 2: *P4, k4, p4, sm, purl to marker, sm, k4, p4, k4.

Row 3: *P4, k4, p4, sm, kfb, knit to marker, kfb, sm, k4, p4, k4—2 stitches increased.

Row 4: *P4, k4, p4, sm, purl to marker, sm, k4, p4, k4.

Row 5: *K4, p4, k4, sm, knit to marker, sm, p4, k4, p4.

Row 6: *K4, p4, k4, sm, purl to marker, sm, p4, k4, p4.

Row 7: *K4, p4, k4, sm, kfb, knit to marker, kfb, sm, p4, k4, p4—2 stitches increased.

Row 8: *K4, p4, k4, sm, purl to marker, sm, p4, k4, p4.

Repeat Rows 1–8 14 (14) more times, then Rows 1–4 0 (1) more times—154 (188) stitches. The hood measures approximately 17 (21)" (43 [53.5]cm) from the setup row.

Divide the stitches evenly onto 2 needles and bind off using the 3-needle bind-off method.

Finishing

Weave in ends. With thread and a sewing needle, attach the buttons, one inside and one outside so that the fabric of the cape overlaps.

Little Red's Basket

With this faux-woven basket, you can carry treats to Granny's house, or simply store some of your yarn stash. Pair it with the Ruby Red Riding Hood (page 10), or make one for Dorothy before she sets out on the Yellow Brick Road. The basket is knitted in a single piece, and needlepoint canvas allows it to hold its shape.

⟻ DESIGNED BY MARILEE NORRIS ⟼

SKILL LEVEL

Intermediate

SIZE

One Size

FINISHED MEASUREMENTS

Approximately 7¼" (18.5cm) square x 5¼" (13.5cm) high, excluding handle

MATERIALS

+ Knit Picks Wool of the Andes Bulky (100% Peruvian highland wool; 3½ oz/100g, 137 yd/126m): 2 skeins in Hazelnut

  (5) BULKY

+ Set of 5 size 8 (5mm) double-pointed needles, or size needed to obtain gauge

+ Size 8 (5mm) 24" circular needle, or size needed to obtain gauge

+ 4 stitch markers

+ Tapestry needle

+ Ruler or tape measure

+ Scissors

+ 5 sheets plastic mesh canvas, 10½" x 13½" (26.5cm x 34.5cm)

+ ¼ yd (23cm) red-and-white checked fabric for lining the basket

+ Fabric-cutting scissors

+ Red thread

+ Sewing needle

+ 2 yd (1.8m) red ribbon, 1½" (3.8cm) wide

GAUGE

18 stitches and 24 rows = 4" (10cm) in stockinette stitch

SPECIAL SKILLS

Knitted cast-on (page 137)

Kitchener stitch (page 137)

STITCH PATTERN

Diamond Basket Pattern

Round 1: *Sm, k4, [p1, k7] 3 times, p1, k3; repeat from * around.

Round 2: *Sm, k3, [p1, k1, p1, k5] 3 times, p1, k1, p1, k2; repeat from * around.

Round 3: *Sm, k2, [p1, k3] 7 times, p1, k1; repeat from * around.

Round 4: *Sm, k1, p1; [k5, p1, k1, p1] 3 times, k5, p1; repeat from * around.

Round 5: *Sm, k8, p1, [k7, p1] 2 times, k7; repeat from * around.

Round 6: Repeat Round 4.

Round 7: Repeat Round 3.

Round 8: Repeat Round 2.

Basket Base

NOTE: The basket is knitted in the round, starting with the base.

Cast on 8 stitches and distribute evenly on double-pointed needles. Switch to the circular needle as needed.

Round 1: *Kfb; repeat from * around—16 stitches.

Round 2: Purl.

Round 3: *Pm, kfb, k2, kfb; repeat from * around—24 stitches.

Round 4: Purl.

Round 5: *Sm, kfb, knit to 1 stitch before the marker, kfb*; repeat from * around—8 stitches increased.

Repeat Rounds 4 and 5 until you have 32 stitches in each section—128 stitches total.

Sides

Work Rounds 1–8 of Diamond Basket Pattern 3 times, then work Rounds 1–4 once more.

Eyelet Round: **Sm, k2tog, yo, k6, p1, *k7, p1*; repeat from * to * until 7 stitches before the marker, k5, yo, ssk; repeat from ** 3 more times.

Work Rounds 6–8 of Diamond Basket Pattern, then work Round 1 once more.

I-cord bind-off: *Remove stitch markers as you come to them.* At the beginning of the round, cast on 3 stitches onto a double-pointed needle using a knitted cast-on. *Slide the stitches to the other end of the needle. K2, k2tog tbl using the last I-cord stitch and the next stitch of the basket. Repeat from * until 3 stitches remain.

K2tog, k1 tbl, transfer these 2 stitches to the left-hand needle, k2tog tbl. Cut yarn, and pull it through this last loop. With Kitchener stitch, seamlessly graft the end of the I-cord bind-off to the beginning of the round.

Handle

Cast on 18 stitches, leaving a long tail for sewing. Place marker and join to knit in the round, being careful not to twist the stitches, and distribute stitches evenly on double-pointed needles.

Round 1: K4, p1, k13.

Round 2: K3, p1, k1, p1, k12.

Round 3: K2, p1, k3, p1, k11.

Round 4: K1, p1, k5, p1, k10.

Round 5: Repeat Round 3.

Round 6: Repeat Round 2.

Repeat these 6 rounds 22 more times, then work Round 1 once more. Bind off, leaving a long tail for sewing.

Finishing

Lay the basket upside down on a flat surface. Measure the base from garter edge to garter edge to determine the size of plastic mesh canvas to cut for the bottom. Cut the plastic mesh square slightly larger than your measurements as the knitted fabric is stretchy. Place the plastic mesh square in the bottom of the basket to check the fit, and cut away any extra little by little as needed.

For the sides, measure the height of the basket to determine the height of the plastic mesh to cut. The width of each side will be the same as the width of the bottom piece. Cut a little more than you think you will need for the height of the side piece. Place the side piece in the basket to check the fit, and cut any extra as needed. Cut three more matching pieces.

To cut fabric for the lining of the basket, use the plastic mesh pieces as a guide. Cut the fabric ½" (13mm) larger than the plastic mesh canvas on all sides. Cut one piece for the bottom of the basket, and four for the sides. Set aside.

Assemble the plastic mesh canvas to create the framework for the basket. Take the base piece and place one of the side pieces on top, lined up along one edge. Thread matching yarn through the mesh holes and sew the two pieces together, preferably with an overcast stitch. Connect the three remaining side pieces in the same manner so all four sides are attached to the bottom plastic mesh piece. Next, fold two adjacent side pieces up, and thread the yarn through the mesh holes to attach the sides of the basket together. Continue until all the sides have been attached and the frame of the basket is complete.

Lay the Handle flat to measure its width. Cut two 13½" (34.5cm) pieces of plastic mesh canvas equal to the width of the Handle. Overlap the ends of the plastic mesh by 2" (5cm). Attach the two pieces together so they create one long piece that is 25" (63.5cm) long. Insert the plastic mesh piece through the center of the knitted Handle; about 2½" (6.5cm) of the plastic mesh will be showing at each end of the Handle. Secure the end of the knitted Handle to the plastic mesh by sewing it in place with the yarn ends.

Place the ends of the Handle on the outside edges of the basket frame so the plastic mesh is flush with the bottom and centered to the frame. Secure in place, leaving the top ½" (13mm) of the Handle unsewn

around the top edge of the basket so the fabric lining can be folded over the edge of the basket. Place the frame inside the knitted basket, and secure it with a few stitches using matching yarn along the bottom of the basket.

Next, sew the fabric lining, constructing it in the same way as the framework for the basket was created. Place the lining in the basket, and fold it over the top of the frame. Sew lining in place along the bottom of the I-cord edge. Finish securing the Handle.

Weave in all ends.

Optional: Add ribbon by threading it through the corners and tie on one side. Go for a walk in the woods with your brand-new basket, stop to pick some flowers for your granny, and don't get fooled by prowling wolves!

Huntsman's Gloves & Scarf

Rustic enough for a huntsman (or huntswoman) preparing for a hard day's work, yet dressy enough for the prince desperately trying to catch that elusive white stag, these gloves and scarf are suitable for any outing. The two-color cuff is knit flat, while the hand is knit in the round. The gloves can be tried on as they are being knit to ensure the perfect length for each finger.

⟻ DESIGNED BY JOAN OF DARK (A.K.A. TONI CARR) ⟼

SKILL LEVEL

Scarf
Easy

Gloves
Intermediate

SIZES

Scarf
One size

Gloves
Women's (Men's)

FINISHED MEASUREMENTS

Scarf
5¾" (14.5cm) wide x 78" (198cm) long

Gloves
Circumference: 8 (9)" (20.5 [23]cm)

MATERIALS

Scarf Only
+ Knit Picks Wool of the Andes (100% wool, 1¾ oz/50g, 110 yd/100m): 2 skeins in Bittersweet Heather (A) **4** MEDIUM

+ Knit Picks Wool of the Andes (100% wool, 1¾ oz/50g, 110 yd/100m): 2 skeins in Mink Heather (B) **4** MEDIUM

Gloves Only
+ Knit Picks Wool of the Andes (100% wool, 1¾ oz/50g, 110 yd/100m): 2 skeins in Bittersweet Heather (A) **4** MEDIUM

+ Knit Picks Wool of the Andes (100% wool, 1¾ oz/50g, 110 yd/100m): 1 skein in Mink Heather (B) **4** MEDIUM

+ Set of 4 size 8 (5mm) double-pointed needles, or size needed to obtain gauge

+ Stitch markers
+ Stitch holders

Both
+ Size 8 (5mm) straight needles, or size needed to obtain gauge

+ Tapestry needle

GAUGE

20 stitches and 26 rows = 4" (10cm) in stockinette stitch

STITCH PATTERN

Linen Stitch
Row 1 (RS): With A, *k1, sl 1 as if to purl, carrying yarn in front; repeat from * to the last 2 stitches, k2.
Row 2: With A, *p1, sl 1 as if to knit, carrying yarn in back; repeat from * to the last 2 stitches, p2.
Row 3: With B, repeat Row 1.
Row 4: With B, repeat Row 2.
Repeat Rows 1–4 for pattern.

Scarf

With A, cast on 38 stitches. Work in linen stitch until piece measures 78" (198cm). Bind off.

FINISHING

Weave in ends. Block firmly.

Gloves
CUFF

With straight needles and A, cast on 44 (48) stitches. Work in Linen Stitch for 4" (10cm), ending with a wrong-side row.

Next row (RS): With A, k1 (2), k2tog, k11 (12), k2tog, k12, k2tog, k11 (12), k2tog, k1 (2)—40 (44) stitches.

Change to double-pointed needles, place marker, and begin working in the round.

Next round: K2tog, knit to last 2 stitches, k2tog—38 (42) stitches.

Knit 3 rounds.

THUMB GUSSET

Left Glove

Next round: K7 (8), place thumb gusset marker, knit to the end of the round.

Next (increase) round: Knit to 1 stitch before thumb gusset marker, M1, k1, sm, k1, M1, knit to the end of the round.

Knit 2 rounds.

Repeat increase round.

Knit 3 rounds.

Next round: Knit to 3 stitches before thumb gusset marker, slip 6 thumb gusset stitches to holder (3 each side of marker), cast on 2 stitches, knit to the end of the round—38 (42) stitches.

Right Glove

K31 (34), place thumb gusset marker, knit to the end of the round.

Next (increase) round: Knit to 1 stitch before thumb gusset marker, M1, k1, sm, k1, M1, knit to the end of the round.

Knit 2 rounds.

Repeat increase round.

Knit 3 rounds.

Next round: Knit to 3 stitches before thumb gusset marker, slip 6 thumb gusset stitches to holder (3 each side of marker), cast on 2 stitches, knit to the end of the round—38 (42) stitches.

BOTH GLOVES

Work even in stockinette stitch for 2 (2½)" (5 [6.5]cm).

Divide stitches evenly onto 2 holders, break yarn.

Begin knitting from the back of stitch holders, starting with pinky finger.

Pinky Finger

Slip 4 (5) stitches from each holder onto working needles. Join new yarn and cast on 1 (2) stitch(es) between pinky finger and stitch holders—9 (12) stitches. Work even for 2 (2¼)" (5 [5.5]cm).

Next round: K1 (0), then k2tog around—5 (6) stitches.

Cut yarn, thread on a tapestry needle, and pull it through the remaining stitches.

Ring Finger

Slip 5 (6) stitches from each stitch holder onto working needles. Join new yarn and cast on 1 stitch between ring and pinky fingers; as you knit around, cast on 1 stitch between ring finger and stitch holders—12 (14) stitches. Work even for 2½ (3)" (6.5 [7.5]cm).

Next round: K2tog around—6 (7) stitches.

Cut yarn, thread on a tapestry needle, and pull it through the remaining stitches.

Middle Finger

Slip 5 stitches from each stitch holder onto working needles. Join new yarn and cast on 1 (2) stitch(es) between ring and middle fingers; as you knit around, cast on 1 stitch between middle finger and stitch holders—12 (13) stitches. Work even for 3 (3½)" (7.5 [9]cm).

Next round: K0 (1), then k2tog around—6 (7) stitches.

Cut yarn, thread on a tapestry needle, and pull it through the remaining stitches.

Index Finger

Place remaining 10 stitches on working needles. Join new yarn and cast on 1 (2) stitches between middle finger and index finger—11 (12) stitches. Work even for 2¼ (2½)" (5.5 [6.5]cm).

Next round: K1 (0), then k2tog around—6 stitches.

Cut yarn, thread on a tapestry needle, and pull it through the remaining stitches.

Thumb

Pick up 5 (6) stitches from the gap, cast on 1 stitch, knit across 6 stitches from the holder—12 (13) stitches. Work even for 2 (2¾)" (5 [7]cm).

Next round: K0 (1), then k2tog around—6 (7) stitches.

Cut yarn, thread on a tapestry needle, and pull it through the remaining stitches.

Finishing

Sew the cuff seam. Weave in ends.

Entwined Forest Throw

Was that a wolf trying to blow your house down? Never fear, it's just the wind howling at your windows. Knit this warm blanket for winter nights to remind you how lucky you are to be safe and sound from the dark creatures lurking in the Enchanted Forest.

DESIGNED BY ABIGAIL HORSFALL

SKILL LEVEL

Intermediate

FINISHED MEASUREMENTS

40" x 47" (101.5cm x 119cm)

MATERIALS

- Knit Picks Swish Worsted (100% superwash merino wool; 1¾ oz/100g, 110 yd/100.5m): 13 balls in Dublin (MC) (4) MEDIUM
- Knit Picks Swish Worsted (100% superwash merino wool; 1¾ oz/100g, 110 yd/100.5m): 8 balls in Bark (CC) (4) MEDIUM
- Size 5 (3.75mm) 40" circular needle, or size needed to obtain gauge
- Cable needle
- Tapestry needle

GAUGE

18 stitches and 36 rows = 4" (10cm) in garter stitch

SPECIAL SKILLS

Cables (page 135)

SPECIAL INSTRUCTIONS

LKl: Lift the stitch 2 rows below the last stitch onto the left-hand needle and knit this stitch.

RKl: Lift the stitch 1 row below the next stitch onto the left-hand needle and knit this stitch.

1/1 LC (rev): Slip 1 stitch to cable needle and hold in front, p1, p1 from cable needle.

1/1 LPC: Slip 1 stitch to cable needle and hold in front, p1, k1 from cable needle.

1/1 RC (rev): Slip 1 stitch to cable needle and hold in back, p1, p1 from cable needle.

1/1 RPC: Slip 1 stitch to cable needle and hold in back, k1, p1 from cable needle.

2/1 LPC: Slip 2 stitches to cable needle and hold in front, p1, k2 from cable needle.

2/1 RPC: Slip 1 stitch to cable needle and hold in back, k2, p1 from cable needle.

2/2 LC: Slip 2 stitches to cable needle and hold in front, k2, k2 from cable needle.

2/2 LPC: Slip 2 stitches to cable needle and hold in front, p2, k2 from cable needle.

2/2 RC: Slip 2 stitches to cable needle and hold in back, k2, k2 from cable needle.

2/2 RPC: Slip 2 stitches to cable needle and hold in back, k2, p2 from cable needle.

NOTE

The blanket is worked in a series of blocks, each building off of the previous block(s) in a log cabin style. Please refer to the diagram (page 25) for clarification of block placement if necessary. All CC blocks are 15 garter ridges (30 rows) tall, and all garter stitch MC blocks are 30 garter ridges (60 rows) tall.

STITCH PATTERN

Tree of Life (multiple of 15 stitches plus 4)

Row 1 (RS): P1, k1, p2, k2, p7, *k2, p4, k2, p7; repeat from * to the last 6 stitches, k2, p2, k1, p1.

Row 2: P1, k3, p2, k7, *p2, k4, p2, k7; repeat from * to the last 6 stitches, p2, k3, p1.

Row 3: P1, k1, p2, 2/1 LPC, p5, *2/1 RPC, p4, 2/1 LPC, p5; repeat from * to the last 7 stitches; 2/1 RPC, p2, k1, p1.

Row 4: P1, k1, p2, k1, p2, k5, p2, k1, *p4, k1, p2, k5, p2, k1; repeat from * to the last 4 stitches, p2, k1, p1.

Row 5: P1, k1, *[2/1 LPC] twice, p3, [2/1 RPC] twice; repeat from * to the last 2 stitches, k1, p1.

Row 6: P1, k2, *p2, k1, p2, k3, p2, k1, p2, k2; repeat from * to the last stitch, p1.

Row 7: P1, k1, p1, [2/1 LPC] twice, p1, [2/1 RPC] twice, *p2, [2/1 LPC] twice, p1, [2/1 RPC] twice; repeat from * to the last 3 stitches, p1, k1, p1.

Row 8: P1, k2, *LKI, k1, p2, k1, p1, p3tog, p1, k1, p2, k1, RKI, k2; repeat from * to the last stitch, p1.

Row 9: P1, k1, p3, 2/1 LPC, k3, 2/1 RPC, *p6, 2/1 LPC, k3, 2/1 RPC; repeat from * to the last 5 stitches, p3, k1, p1.

Row 10: P1, k4, LKI, k1, p2tog, p3, ssp, k1, RKI, *k6, LKI, k1, p2tog, p3, ssp, k1, RKI; repeat from * to the last 5 stitches, k4, p1.

Rows 11 and 13: P1, k1, p5, k5, *p10, k5; repeat from * to the last 7 stitches, p5, k1, p1.

Rows 12 and 14: P1, k6, p5, *k10, p5; repeat from * to the last 7 stitches, k6, p1.

Row 15: P1, k1, p5, k5, *p1, [1/1 LPC, 1/1 RPC] twice, p1, k5; repeat from * to the last 7 stitches, p5, k1, p1.

Row 16: P1, k6, p5, *k2, 1/1 LC (rev), k2, 1/1 RC (rev), k2, p5; repeat from * to the last 7 stitches, k6, p1.

Row 17: P1, k1, p5, k5, *p1, [1/1 RPC, 1/1 LPC] twice, p1, k5; repeat from * to the last 7 stitches, p5, k1, p1.

Row 18: P1, k6, p5, *k1, p1, k2, 1/1 LC (rev), k2, p1, k1, p5; repeat from * to the last 7 stitches, k6, p1.

Rows 19–22: Repeat Rows 15–18.

Row 23: P1, k1, p5, k5, *p1, k1, p6, k1, p1, k5; repeat from * to the last 7 stitches, p5, k1, p1.

Rows 24 and 26: P1, k6, p5, *k10, p5; repeat from * to the last 7 stitches, k6, p1.

Rows 25 and 27: P1, k1, p5, k5, *p10, k5; repeat from * to the last 7 stitches, p5, k1, p1.

Row 28: Repeat Row 24.

Row 29: P1, k1, p3, 2/2 RC, k1, 2/2 LC, *p6, 2/2 RC, k1,

2/2 LC; repeat from * to the last 5 stitches, p3, k1, p1.

Row 30: P1, k4, p9, *k6, p9; repeat from * to the last 5 stitches, k4, p2.

Row 31: P1, k1, p1, 2/2 RPC, k5, 2/2 LPC, *p2, 2/2 RPC, k5, 2/2 LPC; repeat from * to the last 4 stitches, p2, k1, p1.

Row 32: P1, k2, p2, k2, p5, *k2, [p2, k2] twice, p5; repeat from * to the last 7 stitches, k2, p2, k2, p1.

Row 33: P1, k1, *2/1 RPC, 2/2 RC, k1, 2/2 LC, 2/1 LPC; repeat from * to the last 2 stitches, k1, p1.

Row 34: P1, k1, p2, k1, p9, k1, *p4, k1, p9, k1; repeat from * to the last 4 stitches, p2, k1, p1.

Row 35: P1, k3, 2/1 RPC, k5, 2/1 LPC, *2/2 LC, 2/1 RPC, k5, 2/1 LPC; repeat from * to the last 4 stitches, k3, p1.

Row 36: P1, k1, p4, k1, p5, k1, *p8, k1, p5, k1; repeat from * to the last 6 stitches, p4, k1, p1.

Row 37: P1, k1, *2/2 RC, p1, k5, p1, 2/2 RC; repeat from * to the last 2 stitches, k1, p1.

Row 38: P1, k1, ssp, p2, ssp, p3, p2tog, *p2, p2tog, ssp, p2, ssp, p3, p2tog; repeat from * to the last 6 stitches, p4, k1, p1.

Throw

Block 1: Cast on 15 stitches using MC. Work in garter stitch for 30 garter ridges (60 rows), binding off on the final right-side row.

Diagram

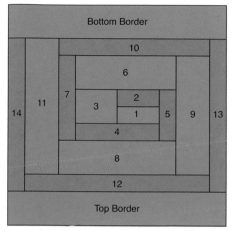

Block 2: Rotate work 90 degrees clockwise and pick up 30 stitches along the side of the block using CC. Work in garter stitch for 15 ridges (30 rows), binding off on the final right-side row.

Block 3: Rotate work 90 degrees clockwise and pick up 30 stitches along the side of the block using MC. Work in garter stitch for 30 ridges (60 rows), binding off on the final right-side row.

Block 4: Rotate work 90 degrees clockwise and pick up 60 stitches along the side of the block using CC. Work in garter stitch for 15 ridges (30 rows), binding off on the final right-side row.

Tree of Life chart

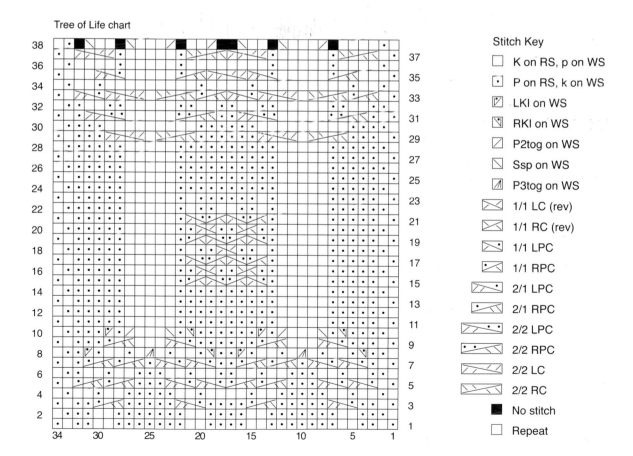

Stitch Key

- ☐ K on RS, p on WS
- ⊡ P on RS, k on WS
- LKI on WS
- RKI on WS
- P2tog on WS
- Ssp on WS
- P3tog on WS
- 1/1 LC (rev)
- 1/1 RC (rev)
- 1/1 LPC
- 1/1 RPC
- 2/1 LPC
- 2/1 RPC
- 2/2 LPC
- 2/2 RPC
- 2/2 LC
- 2/2 RC
- ■ No stitch
- ☐ Repeat

Block 5: Rotate work 90 degrees clockwise and pick up 45 stitches along the side of the block using CC. Work in garter stitch for 15 ridges (30 rows), binding off on the final right-side row.

Block 6: Rotate work 90 degrees clockwise and pick up 75 stitches along the side of the block using MC. Work in garter stitch for 30 ridges (60 rows), binding off on the final right-side row.

Block 7: Rotate work 90 degrees clockwise and pick up 75 stitches along the side of the block using CC. Work in garter stitch for 15 ridges (30 rows), binding off on the final right-side row.

Block 8: Rotate work 90 degrees clockwise and pick up 90 stitches along the side of the block using MC. Work in garter stitch for 30 ridges (60 rows), binding off on the final right-side row.

Block 9: Rotate work 90 degrees clockwise and pick up 105 stitches along the side of the block using MC. Work in garter stitch for 30 ridges (60 rows), binding off on the final right-side row.

Block 10: Rotate work 90 degrees clockwise and pick up 120 stitches along the side of the block using CC. Work in garter stitch for 15 ridges (30 rows), binding off on the final right-side row.

Block 11: Rotate work 90 degrees clockwise and pick up 120 stitches along the side of the block using MC. Work in garter stitch for 30 ridges (60 rows), binding off on the final right-side row.

Block 12: Rotate work 90 degrees clockwise and pick up 150 stitches along the side of the block using CC. Work in garter stitch for 15 ridges (30 rows), binding off on the final right-side row.

Block 13: Rotate work 90 degrees clockwise and pick up 135 stitches along the side of the block using CC. Work in garter stitch for 15 ridges (30 rows), binding off on the final right-side row.

Block 14: Rotate work 180 degrees clockwise and pick up 135 stitches along the side of the block using CC. Work in garter stitch for 15 ridges (30 rows), binding off on the final right-side row.

Top Border: Rotate work 90 degrees clockwise and pick up 184 stitches along the side of the block using MC.

Row 1 (RS): *K1, p1; repeat from * to end.

Row 2: *P1, k1; repeat from * to end.

Repeat these 2 seed-stitch rows 3 more times.

Work 38 rows of Tree of Life Pattern, repeating center panel 11 times total.

Repeat seed-stitch Rows 1 and 2 four times, then bind off loosely.

Bottom Border: Rotate work 180 degrees clockwise and pick up 184 stitches along the side of the block using MC. Repeat Top Border.

Weave in all ends. Wash and block.

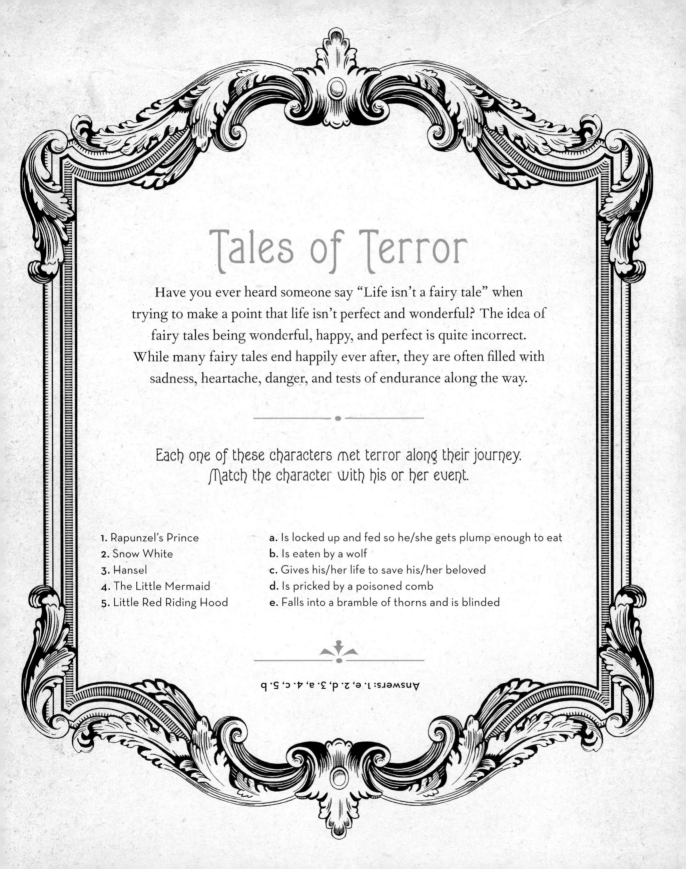

Tales of Terror

Have you ever heard someone say "Life isn't a fairy tale" when trying to make a point that life isn't perfect and wonderful? The idea of fairy tales being wonderful, happy, and perfect is quite incorrect. While many fairy tales end happily ever after, they are often filled with sadness, heartache, danger, and tests of endurance along the way.

Each one of these characters met terror along their journey.
Match the character with his or her event.

1. Rapunzel's Prince
2. Snow White
3. Hansel
4. The Little Mermaid
5. Little Red Riding Hood

a. Is locked up and fed so he/she gets plump enough to eat
b. Is eaten by a wolf
c. Gives his/her life to save his/her beloved
d. Is pricked by a poisoned comb
e. Falls into a bramble of thorns and is blinded

Answers: 1. e, 2. d, 3. a, 4. c, 5. b

Ballerina Fairy Tutu & Wand

Little fairies can romp through the forest (or on their way to ballet class) with this matching skirt and wand dress-up set. These accessories are just as fun to knit as they are to wear, with a self-ruffling ribbon yarn knit doubled for extra frills.

←— DESIGNED BY GENEVIEVE MILLER —→

SKILL LEVEL

Intermediate

SIZES

Child's XS (S, M, L)

FINISHED MEASUREMENTS

Waist: 21 (21½, 23, 24½)"
(53.5 [55, 58.5, 62]cm)

MATERIALS

+ Knit Picks Gloss DK (70% merino, 30% silk; 1¾ oz/50g, 123 yd/112m): 2 (2, 3, 3) skeins in Guava (MC) (3) LIGHT

+ Crystal Palace TuTu (90% acrylic, 10% polyester, 1¾ oz/50g, 34 yd/22m): 2 (2, 3, 3) skeins in 204 Softly Pink (CC)

+ Size 8 (5mm) 24" circular needle, or size needed to obtain gauge

+ Set of 2 size 8 (5mm) double-pointed needles, or size needed to obtain gauge

+ Stitch markers

+ Tapestry needle

+ 1" (2.5cm) non-roll elastic to fit waist (optional)

+ Sewing needle and thread

+ 12" (30.5cm) dowel, ¼" (6mm) in diameter

GAUGE

20 stitches and 28 rows = 4" (10cm) in stockinette stitch with MC

SPECIAL SKILLS

I-cord (page 136)

Skirt

With MC and circular needle, cast on 104 (108, 114, 122) stitches. Place marker and join to work in the round.

Work in k1, p1 rib for 1" (2.5cm).

Work in stockinette stitch for 1" (2.5cm), working last round as follows:

K0 (4, 2, 2), *k13 (13, 14, 15), pm; repeat from * around.

Knit 6 rounds.

Increase Round: K0 (4, 2, 2), *kfb, knit to marker; repeat from * around—8 stitches increased.

Knit 6 rounds.

Repeat the last 7 rounds 4 (5, 6, 7) times more—144 (156, 170, 186) stitches.

Knit 1 round.

Edging

NOTE: See photos for knitting with ruffled yarn (right).

Round 1: With both MC and CC held together, knit.

Round 2: With MC only, work Increase Round.

Repeat the last 2 rounds 4 more times, then work Round 1 once (6 rows of frills).

Bind off with MC. Weave in ends.

Sew elastic to the inside edge of the waist if desired with sewing needle and thread.

1. Pick up the top strand of ruffled yarn, back to front, with the left-hand needle.

2. Insert the right-hand needle into both strands of yarn and knit as usual.

Wand

With MC and double-pointed needles, cast on 5 stitches.

Work I-cord for 11" (28cm).

Rounds 1 and 2: With MC and CC held together, knit. (If you desire a more frilly wand, work every *other* stitch on the CC yarn.)

Round 3: With MC only, *kfb; repeat from *
around—10 stitches.

Repeat Rounds 1 and 2 once more.

With MC only, *k2tog, repeat around.

Knit 1 round.

Bind off. Insert the dowel into the I-cord, sew the
ends closed, and weave in the ends.

Jack and the Bean-socks

Only an incorrigible optimist would trade the family cow for five magic beans! Knit up in a gorgeous multihued green yarn, these socks will keep your feet warm on your next epic journey. Alternating panels of beanstalks and magic beans make them a worthwhile adventure for any daydreamer.

←— DESIGNED BY LAURA HOHMAN —→

SKILL LEVEL

Experienced

SIZES

S (M, L)

FINISHED MEASUREMENTS

6½ (8, 9)" (16.5 [20.5, 23]cm) foot circumference

MATERIALS

◆ Knit Picks Stroll Tonal Sock Yarn (75% superwash merino wool, 25% nylon; 3½ oz/100g, 462 yd/422.5m): 1 (1, 1) skein in Canopy **(1) SUPER FINE**

◆ Set of 5 size 1 (2.25mm) double-pointed needles

◆ Set of 5 size 2 (2.75mm) double-pointed needles, or size needed to obtain gauge

◆ Cable needle

◆ Tapestry needle

GAUGE

32 stitches and 52 rows = 4" (10cm) in stockinette stitch using larger needles

SPECIAL SKILLS

Cables (page 135)

SPECIAL INSTRUCTIONS

B = (Make bobble) Knit in front, back, and front of stitch (3 stitches), turn, p3, turn, k3. With the left-hand needle, pass the second and third stitches over the first stitch.

Toe

With larger needles, cast on 16 (20, 20) stitches. Divide stitches over 3 needles, alternating stitches between needles (first stitch on first needle, second stitch on second needle, third stitch on third needle, etc.).

SETUP ROUND

Needle 1: K4 (5, 5).

Needle 2: K8 (10, 10).

Needle 3: K4 (5, 5).

INCREASE ROUND

Needle 1: Knit to the last stitch, M1, k1.

Needle 2: K1, M1, knit to the last stitch, M1, k1.

Needle 3: K1, M1, knit to end.

Next round: Knit.

Repeat Increase Round every other round 9 (10, 12) times more—56 (64, 72) stitches.

Foot
SETUP ROUND

Needle 1: Knit.

Needle 2: K7 (9, 11), work 14 stitches of Bean and Pea Pattern chart, k7 (9, 11).

Needle 3: Knit.

Work in pattern as established until sock is 3" (7.5cm) less than desired foot length.

GUSSET INCREASE ROUND

Needle 1: Knit to the last stitch, M1, k1.

Needle 2: K7 (9, 11) stitches, work 14 stitches of Bean and Pea Pattern chart, k7 (9, 11).

Needle 3: K1, M1, knit to end.

Continuing in pattern as established, repeat the Gusset Increase Round every other round 8 (9, 10) times more—74 (84, 94) stitches: 23 (26, 29) stitches on each of Needles 1 and 3. Work 1 round even.

Heel

Work back and forth over the first 9 (10, 11) stitches of Needle 1 and the last 9 (10, 11) stitches of Needle 3 with a spare needle as follows:

K7 (8, 9), kfb, k1, turn.

Sl 1, p16 (18, 20), pfb, p1, turn.

Sl 1, knit to last 3 stitches, kfb, k1, turn.

Sl 1, purl to last 3 stitches, pfb, p1, turn.

Sl 1, knit to last 5 stitches, kfb, k1, turn.

Sl 1, purl to last 5 stitches, pfb, p1, turn.

Continue increasing the heel, always working an increase in the stitch right before the previous increase, until there are 28 (32, 36) stitches on the needle. *Do not turn* after the last purl increase row. Purl to the last stitch, purl the last stitch together with a stitch from next needle, turn.

Row 1: *Sl 1, k1; repeat from * to the last stitch, skp the last stitch with a stitch from the next needle, turn.

Row 2: Sl 1, purl to the last stitch, purl the last stitch together with a stitch from the next needle, turn.

Repeat these 2 rows until all the gusset stitches have been worked, ending with a Row 1 skp. You should now have 56 (64, 72) stitches total. Begin working in the round again.

Leg
SETUP ROUND

Needle 1: K7 (9, 11), work 14 stitches of Bean and Pea Pattern chart (continuing pattern from the instep).

Needle 2: P0 (2, 4), work 14 stitches in 5-Braid Cable pattern, p0 (2, 4).

Needle 3: Work 14 stitches in Bean and Pea Pattern chart.

Needle 4: P0 (2, 4), using stitches from Needle 1 work 14 stitches in 5-Braid Cable pattern, p0 (2, 4).

Work in patterns as established until leg measures 5" (12.5cm) from the top of the heel flap.

Cuff
Switch to smaller needles. Work in k1, p1 rib for 1" (2.5cm). Bind off.

Finishing
Use a tapestry needle to weave in the ends.

Repeat pattern to make a matching sock.

Bean and Pea Pattern

5-Braid Cable Pattern

Stitch Key

☐	Knit
·	Purl
ℓ	K1 tbl
○	Yo
B	Make bobble
◿	K2tog
◺	Ssk
⬳	C5B
⬳	C5F
☐	Repeat

Yellow Brick Road Bag

Follow the Yellow Brick Road—and this interesting stitch pattern—to create a cozy bag that can be customized to fit nearly any size laptop or tablet. It will keep your treasured device safe from flying monkeys, angry orchards, and even the Wicked Witch of the West!

←—— DESIGNED BY GENEVIEVE MILLER ——→

SKILL LEVEL

Intermediate

SIZES

S (M, L)

FINISHED MEASUREMENTS

Width: 13 (15, 17)" (33 [38, 43]cm)

Height: 9 (10, 10¾)" (23 [25.5, 27.5]cm)

Depth: 1 (1, 1)" (2.5 [2.5, 2.5]cm)

MATERIALS

◆ Knit Picks Brava Worsted (100% acrylic, 3½ oz/100g, 218 yd/199.3m): 2 skeins in Canary (MC) **(4) MEDIUM**

◆ Knit Picks Brava Worsted (100% acrylic, 3½ oz/100g, 218 yd/199.3m): 1 skein in Cobblestone Heather (CC) **(4) MEDIUM**

◆ Size 7 (4.5mm) 24" circular needle, or size needed to obtain gauge

◆ Tapestry needle

◆ 2 buttons, 1" (2.5cm) in diameter

◆ Heavy fabric for lining (optional)

◆ Matching thread and sewing needle (optional)

GAUGE

20 stitches and 36 rows = 4" (10cm) in pattern

Row 10: P2, *sl 1 knitwise wyib, p4; repeat from * to the last 3 stitches, sl 1 knitwise wyib, p2.

Row 11: K2, *sl 1 purlwise wyif, k4; repeat from * to the last 3 stitches, sl 1 purlwise wyif, k2.

Row 12: Repeat Row 10.

Repeat these 12 rows until piece measures approximately 22½ (24½, 26)" (57 [62, 66]cm) from the cast-on edge, ending with Row 1 or Row 7 of the pattern.

Buttonholes

Row 1 (Row 2 or Row 8 of the pattern): With CC, k19 (24, 29), bind off 4 stitches, p18, bind off 4 stitches, knit to end.

Row 2: Change to MC. Work Row 3 or Row 9 of the pattern as established, casting on 4 stitches over the previously bound-off stitches.

Work 11 more rows in pattern (to complete 2 rows of bricks), ending with Row 2 or Row 8 of the pattern. With CC, bind off knitwise.

Side Panels (make 2)

With CC, cast on 7 stitches.

Row 1: Sl 1 knitwise, knit to end.

Row 2: Sl 1 knitwise, purl to end.

Repeat these 2 rows until the piece measures 9 (10, 10¾)" (23 [25.5, 27.5]cm) from the cast-on edge. Bind off.

Bag

With CC, cast on 65 (75, 85) stitches.

Row 1 (WS): Purl.

Row 2: Knit.

Row 3: Change to MC. *P4, sl 1 purlwise wyif; repeat from * to end.

Row 4: *Sl 1 knitwise wyib, p4; repeat from * to end.

Row 5: *K4, sl 1 purlwise wyif; repeat from * to end.

Row 6: Repeat Row 4.

Row 7: Change to CC. Purl.

Row 8: Knit.

Row 9: Change to MC. P2, *sl 1 purlwise wyif, p4; repeat from * to the last 3 stitches, sl 1 purlwise wyif, p2.

Strap

With CC, cast on 9 stitches.

Row 1 (WS): With CC, purl.

Row 2: Knit.

Row 3: Change to MC, p2, sl 1 purlwise wyif, p4, sl 1 purlwise wyif, p1.

Row 4: P1, sl 1 knitwise wyib, p4, sl 1 knitwise wyib, p2.

Row 5: K2, sl 1 purlwise wyif, k4, sl 1 purlwise wyif, k1.

Row 6: Repeat Row 4.

Row 7: With CC, purl.

Row 8: Knit.

Row 9: Change to MC. P4, sl 1 purlwise wyif, p4.

Row 10: P4, sl 1 knitwise wyib, p4.

Row 11: K4, sl 1 purlwise wyif, k4.

Row 12: Repeat Row 10.

Repeat these 12 rows until the Strap measures approximately 34" (86cm) or desired length, ending with Row 2 or Row 8. Bind off with CC.

Finishing

Block pieces to measurements. Weave in ends. Sew Side Panels to the body of the bag, starting at the inside front edge and working around to the flap, making sure you have the same number of bricks on the front as on the back. Sew the ends of the Strap to the Side Panels. Sew on buttons.

Make lining, if desired, and sew into bag and to the wrong side of the Strap. To line, cut a piece of fabric a bit smaller than the knitted piece, leaving ¼" on each side and 2" at the top, by the buttonholes. With a needle and thread to match the lining, sew the fabric to the wrong side of the piece. Repeat to create a lining for the strap.

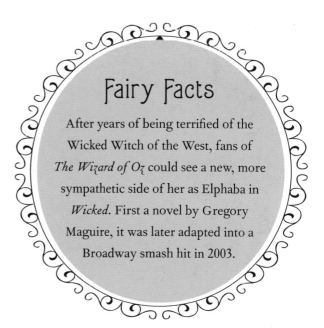

Fairy Facts

After years of being terrified of the Wicked Witch of the West, fans of *The Wizard of Oz* could see a new, more sympathetic side of her as Elphaba in *Wicked*. First a novel by Gregory Maguire, it was later adapted into a Broadway smash hit in 2003.

Woodland Friends Hats

You'll find all sorts of creatures in the Enchanted Forest.
Are they friend or foe? Transform yourself into your favorite
fairy-tale animal with these modern, slouchy hats, customized
for clever pigs, cunning wolves, and amiable bears.

—← DESIGNED BY GENEVIEVE MILLER →—

SKILL LEVEL

Easy

SIZES

Small (Large)

FINISHED MEASUREMENTS

20 (21½)" (51 [55]cm) in
circumference

MATERIALS

For All Versions

+ Size 11 (8mm) 16" circular
  needle, or size needed to
  obtain gauge

+ Size 13 (9mm) 16" circular
  needle, or size needed to
  obtain gauge

+ Set of size 13 (9mm) double-
  pointed needles, or size
  needed to obtain gauge

+ Stitch marker

+ Tapestry needle

Bear Version

+ Knit Picks Biggo (50%
  superwash merino wool, 50%
  nylon; 3½ oz/100g,
  110 yd/100m): 1 skein in
  Reindeer Heather **5 BULKY**

Wolf Version

+ Knit Picks Biggo (50%
  superwash merino wool,
  50% nylon; 3½ oz/100g,
  110 yd/100.5m): 1 skein in
  Cobblestone Heather
  5 BULKY

Pig Version

+ Knit Picks Biggo (50%
  superwash merino wool,
  50% nylon; 3½ oz/100g,
  110 yd/100.5m): 1 skein in
  Dogwood Heather **b BULKY**

GAUGE

12 stitches and 17 rows = 4" (10cm)
in stockinette stitch using larger
needles

12 stitches and 17 rows = 4" (10cm)
in k1, p1 rib (slightly stretched)
using smaller needles

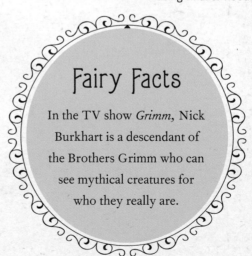

Fairy Facts

In the TV show *Grimm*, Nick
Burkhart is a descendant of
the Brothers Grimm who can
see mythical creatures for
who they really are.

Hat

With smaller needle and desired color, cast on 60 (64) stitches. Place marker and join to work in the round.

Work in k1, p1 rib for 1" (2.5cm).

Switch to larger needles.

Work in stockinette stitch until the hat measures 5 (6)" (12.5 [15]cm) from cast-on edge. Switch to double-pointed needles when necessary.

CROWN DECREASES

Round 1: *K2tog, k8 (6); repeat from * around—54 (56) stitches.

Round 2: *K2tog, k7 (5); repeat from * around—48 (48) stitches.

Round 3: *K2tog, k6 (4); repeat from * around—42 (40) stitches.

Round 4: *K2tog, k5 (3); repeat from * around—36 (32) stitches.

Round 5: *K2tog, k4 (2); repeat from * around—30 (24) stitches.

Round 6: *K2tog, k3 (1); repeat from * around—24 (16) stitches.

Round 7: *K2tog, k2 (0); repeat from * around—18 (8) stitches.

Round 8: *K2tog; repeat from * around—9 (4) stitches.

Cut yarn, leaving a long tail. Thread tail through all stitches, pull tightly, and weave in the end.

Bear Ears (make 4)

With larger needle, cast on 8 stitches.

Rows 1 and 3 (RS): Knit.

Rows 2 and 4: Purl.

Row 5: Kfb, k6, kfb—10 stitches.

Row 6: Purl.

Bind off and weave in ends. The cast-on row will be the top of the ear. Tuck in sides so the ear curves slightly at the top.

With wrong sides together, sew each pair of ears together and attach to the top of the hat.

Wolf or Pig Ears (make 4)

With larger needles and desired color, cast on 12 stitches.

Row 1 (RS): Knit.

Rows 2, 4, 6, 8, and 10: Purl.

Row 3: Ssk, k8, k2tog—10 stitches.

Row 5: Ssk, k6, k2tog—8 stitches.

Row 7: Ssk, k4, k2tog—6 stitches.

Row 9: Ssk, k2, k2tog—4 stitches.

Row 11: Ssk, k2tog—2 stitches.

Row 12: P2tog—1 stitch.

Cut yarn and pull the end through the last stitch.

With wrong sides together, sew each pair of ears together and attach to the top of the hat.

Princes & Princesses

Long ago, in a faraway land, princes and princesses had a knack for getting themselves into trouble. Dark forces threatened royal babies with sleeping curses, innocent young ladies with poisoned apples, and handsome princes with spells that turned them into hideous beasts. Even in fairy tales, happy endings had to be earned through trials and tribulations.

If you dream of slaying (or befriending) dragons, rescuing damsels in distress, or meeting Prince Charming, look no further than these regal projects. Tiny princesses will love a snuggly blanket adorned with flowers, a charming party hat, and a girly, swirly skirt with a matching top. Noble ladies can choose from a stunning pair of cropped sweaters, rose-adorned wristlets, or a shawlette to channel their inner mermaid. And a modern princely cardigan will suit your brave knight perfectly.

Siren Shawl

You'll feel like you're dancing on the ocean floor when you wrap yourself in this Estonian lace pattern with nupps that mimics seaweed. Beginning with a picot cast-on, the body is worked from the bottom up in short rows; a row of eyelets completes the top edge. It's a treasure fit for a mermaid.

← DESIGNED BY CASSIE CASTILLO →

SKILL LEVEL

Intermediate

SIZE

One size

FINISHED MEASUREMENTS

Width: 58" (147 cm)

Length at center: 14" (35.5cm)

MATERIALS

◆ Madelinetosh Tosh Merino Light (100% superwash merino wool, 3½ oz/100g) 420 yd/384m): 2 skeins in Baltic

1 SUPER FINE

◆ Size 6 (4mm) knitting needles, or size needed to obtain gauge

◆ Tapestry needle

◆ Blocking pins

GAUGE

18 stitches and 32 rows = 4" (10cm) in stockinette stitch

SPECIAL SKILLS

Short rows (page 139)

SPECIAL INSTRUCTIONS

Nupp: K1, [yo, k1] 3 times in the same stitch to make 7 stitches. These 7 stitches are purled together on the next row.

P7tog: Purl 7 stitches together.

STITCH PATTERN

Seaweed Lace (multiple of 9 stitches plus 5)
Row 1 (RS): K1, k2tog, *yo, k1, nupp, k1, yo, k1, ssk, k2tog, k1; repeat from * to the last 2 stitches, yo, k2.
Row 2 (WS): P3, *p6, p7tog, p2; repeat from * to the last 2 stitches, p2.

Row 3: K2, *k1, k2tog, [k1, yo] twice, k1, ssk, k1; repeat from * to the last 3 stitches, k3.
Row 4: Purl.
Row 5: K2, *k2tog, k1, yo, k1, nupp, k1, yo, k1, ssk; repeat from * to the last 3 stitches, k3.
Row 6: P3, *p4, p7tog, p4; repeat from * to the last 2 stitches, p2.
Row 7: K1, k2tog, *[k1, yo] twice, k1, ssk, k2, k2tog; repeat from * to the last 2 stitches, yo, k2.
Row 8: Purl.
Repeat Rows 1–8 for pattern.

NOTES

After working a nupp, stretch the stitches on the needle, which makes them all an even length. This will make the stitches easier to purl together on the next row.

To make a yarn over after a purl stitch, wrap the yarn around the needle from front to back until the yarn is at the front of the work again.

Repeat Short Rows 3 and 4 until all the stitches have been worked—235 stitches.

Purl 2 rows.

Next row (RS): P1, *p2tog, yo; repeat from * to the last 2 stitches, p2.

Knit 3 rows.

Bind off all stitches.

Finishing

Weave in ends. Block to finished measurements with blocking pins.

Fairy Facts

Disney's *Little Mermaid* gave the heroine a happy ending, which is the opposite of Hans Christian Andersen's original tale.

Shawl

Make a slipknot and place it on the left-hand needle. *Cast on 4 stitches (excluding stitches already on the left-hand needle) with a knitted cast-on. Bind off 2 stitches. Slip the stitch on the right-hand needle to the left-hand needle; repeat from * until there are 311 stitches on the left-hand needle.

Work Rows 1–8 of Seaweed Lace 3 times.

Purl 2 rows.

Next row (RS): P1, *p2tog, yo; repeat from * to the last 2 stitches, p2.

Knit 1 row.

Short Row 1: K159, turn.

Short Row 2: P7, turn.

Short Row 3: Knit to 1 stitch before the gap, ssk, k3, turn.

Short Row 4: Purl to 1 stitch before the gap, p2tog, p3, turn.

Briar Rose's Blanket

Newborn princesses deserve only the finest gifts from their fairy godmothers. Embellish this incredibly soft blanket with flowers blossoming from intertwined cables inspired by the baby heroine of *Sleeping Beauty*, named after such flowers in the Brothers Grimm version *Little Briar Rose*.

←— DESIGNED BY GENEVIEVE MILLER —→

SKILL LEVEL

Intermediate

SIZE

Approximately 38½" x 39" (98cm x 99cm)

MATERIALS

◆ Knit Picks Comfy Worsted (75% pima cotton, 25% acrylic; 1¾ oz/50g, 109 yd/99.7 m): 9 skeins in 25770 Zinnia (MC) (4) MEDIUM

◆ Knit Picks Comfy Worsted (75% pima cotton, 25% acrylic; 1¾ oz/50g, 109 yd/99.7 m): 3 skeins in 25313 Fairy Tale (CC) (4) MEDIUM

◆ Size 7 (4.5mm) 32" or 40" circular needle, or size needed to obtain gauge

◆ 6 stitch markers

◆ Cable needle

◆ Tapestry needle

◆ Embroidery needle and light-colored floss

GAUGE

19 stitches and 24 rows = 4" (10cm) in seed stitch

19 stitches and 27 rows = 4" (10cm) in reverse stockinette stitch

SPECIAL SKILLS

Cables (page 135)

Embroidery stitches (page 136)

SPECIAL INSTRUCTIONS

RC RS: Slip 2 stitches to cable needle and hold in back, p4, k2, k2 from cable needle.

RC WS: Slip 2 stitches to cable needle and hold in back, p2, k4, p2 from cable needle.

LC RS: Slip 2 stitches to cable needle and hold in front, p4, k2, k2 from cable needle.

LC WS: Slip 2 stitches to cable needle and hold in front, p2, k4, p2 from cable needle.

STITCH PATTERN

Seed stitch (over an even number of stitches)
Row 1 (RS): *K1, p1; repeat from * to end.
Row 2: *P1, k1; repeat from * to end.
Repeat Rows 1 and 2 for pattern.

Blanket

With CC, cast on 160 stitches.

Work 15 rows in seed stitch, ending with a right-side row.

Change to MC. Purl 1 wrong-side row.

Work 11 rows in reverse stockinette stitch (purl on right side, knit on wrong side).

CABLES

Row 1 (RS): P16, pm, k2, p4, k2, pm, p52, pm, k2, p4, k2, pm, p52, pm, k2, p4, k2, pm, p16.

Row 2: Knit to marker, p2, k4, p2, knit to marker, p2, k4, p2, knit to marker, p2, k4, p2, knit to end.

Rows 3–6: Repeat Rows 1 and 2.

Row 7: Purl to marker, RC RS, purl to marker, LC RS, purl to marker, RC RS, purl to the end.

Row 8: Knit to marker, RC WS, knit to marker, LC WS, knit to marker, RC WS, knit to the end.

Rows 9–24: Repeat Rows 1 and 2.

Rows 25 and 26: Repeat Rows 7 and 8.

Rows 27–48: Repeat Rows 1 and 2.

Rows 49 and 50: Repeat Rows 7 and 8.

Rows 51–58: Repeat Rows 1 and 2.

Rows 59 and 60: Repeat Rows 7 and 8.

Rows 61–68: Repeat Rows 1 and 2.

Row 69: *Purl to marker, LC RS; repeat from * twice more, purl to end.

Row 70: *Knit to marker, LC WS; repeat from * twice more, knit to end.

Rows 71–92: Repeat Rows 1 and 2.

Rows 93 and 94: Repeat Rows 69 and 70.

Rows 95–102: Repeat Rows 1 and 2.

Rows 103 and 104: Repeat Rows 69 and 70.

Rows 105–112: Repeat Rows 1 and 2.

Rows 113 and 114: Repeat Rows 69 and 70.

Rows 115–136: Repeat Rows 1 and 2.

Rows 137 and 138: Repeat Rows 7 and 8.

Rows 139–146: Repeat Rows 1 and 2.

Rows 147 and 148: Repeat Rows 7 and 8.

Rows 149–156: Repeat Rows 1 and 2.

Rows 157 and 158: Repeat Rows 7 and 8.

Rows 159–180: Repeat Rows 1 and 2.

Rows 181 and 182: Repeat Rows 7 and 8.

Rows 183–198: Repeat Rows 1 and 2.

Rows 199 and 200: Repeat Rows 7 and 8.

Rows 201–206: Repeat Rows 1 and 2.

Work 11 rows in reverse stockinette stitch.

Change to CC. Purl 1 wrong-side row.

Work 15 rows in seed stitch.

Bind off all stitches in pattern.

SIDE BORDERS

With the right side facing and CC, pick up 184 stitches evenly across the entire length of the blanket. Work 15 rows in seed stitch.

Bind off all stitches in pattern. Repeat on the other side.

Weave in all ends and block lightly to open up the cables.

Flowers (make 6)
PETALS (MAKE 5 FOR EACH FLOWER)

With CC, cast on 2 stitches.

Row 1: Knit.

Row 2 and all WS rows: Purl.

Row 3: Kfb, kfb—4 stitches.

Row 5: Kfb, k2, kfb—6 stitches.

Row 7: kfb, k4 kfb—8 stitches.

Row 9: Knit.

Row 10: Bind off all stitches purlwise.

Sew 5 petals together, then sew them onto the blanket at the cable crossings to form each flower. With contrasting colored yarn or embroidery floss, embroider the center of the flowers with satin stitch.

Snow White Shrug

Did you know there are two fairy-tale heroines called Snow White?
Both stories include dwarfs, but with very different dispositions.
One Snow White is the sister of Rose Red, and her cropped
sweater, with ruffles and a simple lace heart pattern,
is a slightly sweeter take on the Rose Red Wrap (page 60).

←— DESIGNED BY JOAN OF DARK (A.K.A. TONI CARR) —→

SKILL LEVEL

Intermediate

SIZES

S (M, L, XL)

FINISHED MEASUREMENTS

Back width at underarm: 21¼
(22½, 24½, 26¾)" (54 [57, 62, 68]
cm)

Length from back neck to
point (excluding edging): 21¼
(22¼, 23½, 24¼)" (54 [56.5, 59.5,
61.5]cm)

MATERIALS

◆ Plymouth Yarn Galway
Worsted (100% wool,
3½ oz/100g), 210yd/100.5m:
3 (3, 4, 4) skeins in Bleach
(4) MEDIUM

◆ Size 9 (5mm) 40" circular
needle, or size needed to
obtain gauge

◆ Set of 5 size 9 (5mm) double-
pointed needles, or size
needed to obtain gauge

◆ 2 stitch markers

◆ Tapestry needle

GAUGE

15 stitches and 23 rows = 4" (10cm)
in stockinette stitch

STITCH PATTERN

**Lace Heart Pattern (worked
over 14 stitches)**
Row 1 (RS): K6, yo, ssk, k6.
Row 2 and all WS rows: Purl.
Row 3: K4, k2tog, yo, k1, yo,
ssk, k5.
Row 5: K3, k2tog, yo, k3, yo,
ssk, k4.
Row 7: K2, k2tog, yo, k5, yo,
ssk, k3.
Row 9: K1, k2tog, yo, k7, yo,
ssk, k2.
Row 11: K2tog, yo, k4, yo, ssk, k3,
yo, ssk, k1.
Row 13: K1, yo, ssk, k1, k2tog, yo,
k1, yo, ssk, k1, k2tog, yo, k2.
Row 15: K2, yo, sk2p, yo, k3, yo,
sk2p, yo, k3.
Row 16: Purl.

Back

With the circular needle, cast on 2 stitches.

Row 1 (WS): Purl.

Row 2: [Kfb] twice—4 stitches.

Row 3: Pfb, purl to the last stitch, pfb—6 stitches.

Row 4: Kfb, knit to the last stitch, kfb—8 stitches.

Repeat Rows 3 and 4 until there are 24 (28, 36, 44) stitches on the needle, ending with Row 4.

Setup row: Pfb, p4 (6, 10, 14), pm, p14, pm, purl to the last stitch, pfb—26 (30, 38, 46) stitches.

Continue increasing as established, slipping markers and working the Lace Heart pattern between markers over the next 16 rows, until there are 66 (70, 78, 88) stitches on the needle, ending with a right-side row.

Continuing in stockinette stitch, repeat Row 4 every right-side row 4 times—74 (78, 86, 94) stitches.

Continue increasing on right-side rows as established, working Lace Heart pattern between markers, until there are 80 (84, 92, 100) stitches on the needle.

Continuing even in stockinette stitch, complete Lace Heart pattern.

Work 12 rows even in stockinette stitch.

Continue increasing on right-side rows as before, working Lace Heart pattern between markers, until there are 96 (100, 108, 116) stitches on the needle, ending with a wrong-side row.

Next row: Repeat Row 4—98 (102, 110, 118) stitches.

Next row: Repeat Row 3—100 (104, 112, 120) stitches.

Sleeves

Next row: Cast on 18 (18, 20, 20) stitches, knit the cast-on stitches, and knit to end.

Next row: Cast on 18 (18, 20, 20) stitches, purl the cast-on stitches, and purl to end—136 (140, 152, 160) stitches.

Work 8 rows even in stockinette stitch.

Continuing even in stockinette stitch, work 16 rows of Lace Heart pattern between markers.

Remove markers and work even in stockinette stitch until sleeves measure 5½ (6, 7, 7)" (14 [15, 18, 18]cm) from sleeve cast-on, ending with a wrong-side row.

Neck

Next row (RS): K54 (55, 60, 64) , join a second ball of yarn, bind off the center 28 (30, 32, 32) stitches, knit to end—54 (55, 60, 64) stitches on each side.

Work even in stockinette stitch on both sides until sleeves measure 10½ (11, 13½, 13½)" (26.5 [28, 34.5, 34.5]cm) from the sleeve cast-on, ending with a wrong-side row.

Shape Fronts
RIGHT FRONT

Row 1 (RS): K2tog, knit to end—53 (54, 59, 63) stitches.

Row 2: Purl.

Rows 3–15: Repeat Rows 1 and 2—46 (47, 52, 56) stitches after Row 15.

Row 16: Bind off 18 (18, 20, 20) stitches, purl to end—28 (29, 32, 36) stitches.

Row 17: K2tog, knit to end—27 (29, 32, 36) stitches.

Row 18: Bind off 8 (8, 10, 10) stitches, purl to end—20 (21, 22, 26) stitches.

Bind off the remaining stitches.

LEFT FRONT

Row 1 (RS): Knit to the last 2 stitches, ssk—53 (54, 59, 63) stitches.

Row 2: Purl.

Rows 3–16: Repeat Rows 1 and 2—46 (47, 52, 56) stitches after Row 15.

Row 17: Bind off 18 (18, 20, 20) stitches, knit to last 2 stitches, ssk—27 (29, 32, 36) stitches.

Row 18: Purl.

Row 19: Bind off 8 (8, 10, 10) stitches, knit to end—20 (21, 22, 26) stitches.

Bind off the remaining stitches.

Finishing

Fold sleeves over and sew sleeve and side seams.

BODY AND NECK EDGING

With circular needle, pick up 210 (216, 220, 224) stitches evenly around entire neck and body edge of shrug. Place marker and join for working in the round.

Round 1: Knit.

Round 2: *Kfb; repeat from * around—420 (432, 440, 448) stitches.

Rounds 3 and 4: Knit.

Round 5: *K1, kfb; repeat from * around—630 (648, 660, 672) stitches.

Round 6: Knit.

Bind off.

SLEEVE EDGING

NOTE: With the large number of increases and stitches, using a 40" circular needle and the Magic Loop (see page 137) method may be easier than using double-pointed needles.

With double-pointed needles, pick up 62 (62, 72, 72) stitches. Place marker and join for working in the round.

Round 1: Knit.

Round 2: *Kfb; repeat from * around—124 (124, 144, 144) stitches.

Rounds 3 and 4: Knit.

Round 5: *K1, kfb; repeat from * around—186 (186, 216, 216) stitches.

Round 6: Knit.

Bind off.

Weave in all ends and block lightly.

Charming Cardigan

I confess that I'm a sucker for a happy ending. And while I didn't always subscribe to the idea that a knight on a white horse would sweep me off my feet, I have found Snow White's Charming to be quite like his name. This sweater is inspired by the leather jacket he wears in the Enchanted Forest in *Once Upon a Time*.

←— DESIGNED BY GENEVIEVE MILLER —→

SKILL LEVEL

Intermediate

SIZES

Men's S (M, L, XL)

FINISHED MEASUREMENTS

Chest: 36 (40, 44, 48)" (91 [101.5, 112, 122]cm)

Length: 24 (25, 26, 27)" (61 [63.5, 66, 68.5]cm)

Sleeves to underarm: 19 (20, 21, 22)" (48.5 [51, 53.5, 56]cm)

MATERIALS

✦ Brown Sheep Nature Spun Worsted (100% wool, 3½ oz/100g, 245 yd/224m): 8 (9, 10, 11) skeins in Roasted Coffee (A) (4) MEDIUM

✦ Brown Sheep Nature Spun Worsted (100% wool, 3½ oz/100g, 245 yd/224m): 1 skein in Scarlet (B) (4) MEDIUM

✦ Size 7 (4.5mm) 32" circular needle, or size needed to obtain gauge

✦ Set of 2 size 7 (4.5mm) double-pointed needles, or size needed to obtain gauge

✦ Cable needle

✦ Tapestry needle

✦ Zipper, 26 (27, 28, 29)" (66 [68.5, 71, 74]cm) long

✦ Sewing needle and thread

GAUGE

28 stitches and 24 rows = 4" (10cm) in rib pattern, unstretched

24 stitches and 24 rows = 4" (10cm) in rib pattern, after blocking

SPECIAL SKILLS

Cables (page 135)

I-cord (page 136)

SPECIAL INSTRUCTIONS

C4B: Place 2 stitches on cable needle and hold to the back, k2, k2 from the cable needle.

C4F: Place 2 stitches on cable needle and hold to the front, k2, k2 from the cable needle.

As you change colors in the contrast cable, wrap the yarn not being used around the working yarn to keep it secure.

Back

With A, cast on 110 (120, 130, 142) stitches. Work in k1, p1 rib until piece measures 15 (15½, 16, 16½)" (38 [39.5, 40.5, 42]cm), ending with a wrong-side row.

SHAPE ARMHOLES

Working in rib pattern as set, bind off 5 (6, 7, 8) stitches at beginning of next 2 rows. Bind off 3 stitches at beginning of following 2 rows. Bind off 1 stitch at beginning of next 4 rows—90 (98, 106, 116) stitches.

Work even in pattern until armhole measures 9 (9½, 10, 10½)" (23 [24, 25.5, 26.5]cm), ending with a wrong-side row.

SHAPE SHOULDERS

Working in rib pattern as set, bind off 5 (6, 6, 7) stitches at beginning of next 2 rows. Bind off 7 (7, 7, 8) stitches at beginning of following 2 rows. Bind off 5 (5, 6, 6) stitches at beginning of next 2 rows—17 (18, 19, 21) stitches per shoulder.

Bind off all remaining stitches in pattern.

Right Front

With A, cast on 55 (60, 65, 71) stitches.

Work in k1, p1 rib, slipping the first stitch purlwise of each right-side row (center front edge). Work even for 2" (5cm), ending with a wrong-side row.

BEGIN CABLE

Row 1 (RS): With A, sl 1, k1, p1, k1, p1; with B, C4F; with A, work as established to end.

Rows 2, 4, and 6: With A, work in pattern to cable stitches; with B, p4 across cable; with A, work as established to end.

Rows 3 and 5: With A, sl 1, k1, p1, k1, p1; with B, k4; with A, work as set to end.

Repeat Rows 1–6 thirteen times, then work even with A and k1, p1 rib until piece measures same as Back to armholes, ending with a right-side row.

SHAPE ARMHOLE

Working in rib pattern as set, bind off 5 (6, 7, 8) stitches at beginning of next wrong-side row. Bind off 3 stitches at beginning of following wrong-side row. Bind off 1 stitch at beginning of the next 2 wrong-side rows—45 (49, 53, 58) stitches.

Work even until armhole measures 6 (6½, 7, 7½)" (15 [16.5, 18, 19]cm), ending with a wrong-side row.

SHAPE NECK

Bind off 11 (13, 15, 17) stitches at beginning of the next right-side row. Bind off 5 (6, 7, 8) stitches at beginning of the following right-side row. Bind off 3 stitches at the beginning of the next 2 right-side rows. Bind off 2 stitches at the beginning of the next 3 right-side rows—17 (18, 19, 21) stitches. Work even until armhole measures same as Back to shoulder shaping, ending with a right-side row.

SHAPE SHOULDER

Bind off 5 (6, 6, 7) stitches at the beginning of the next wrong-side row. Bind off 7 (7, 7, 8) stitches at the beginning of the following wrong-side row. Bind off 5 (5, 6, 6) stitches at the beginning of the next wrong-side row.

Left Front

Work as for the Right Front, slipping the first stitch of each wrong-side row, until the start of the cable.

BEGIN CABLE

Row 1 (RS): With A, work in pattern to last 9 stitches; with B, C4B; with A, work as established to end.

Rows 2, 4, and 6: With A, sl 1, work in pattern to cable stitches; with B, p4 across cable; with A, work as set to end.

Rows 3 and 5: With A, work in pattern to last 9 stitches; with B, k4; with A, work as set to end.

Repeat Rows 1–6 thirteen times, then work even with A and k1, p1 rib until piece measures same as Back to the armholes, ending with a wrong-side row.

SHAPE ARMHOLE

Work as for the Right Front, binding off at the beginning of right-side rows.

SHAPE NECK

Work as for the Right Front, binding off at the beginning of wrong-side rows.

SHAPE SHOULDER

Work as for the Right Front, binding off at the beginning of right-side rows.

Sleeves (make 2)

Cast on 60 stitches. Work in k1, p1 rib for 2" (5cm).

Increase 1 stitch at each end of the row every 6 rows 13 (14, 15, 16) times, then every 4 rows 4 (5, 7, 9) times—94 (98, 104, 110) stitches. Work even until the piece measures 19 (20, 21, 22)" (48.5 [51, 53.5, 56]cm), ending with a wrong-side row.

SHAPE CAP

Bind off 5 (6, 7, 8) stitches at the beginning of the next 2 rows. Bind off 3 stitches at the beginning of the next 2 rows—78 (80, 84, 88) stitches. Decrease 1 stitch at each end of every other row 5 times, then at each end of every row until 16 stitches remain. Bind off 2 stitches at the beginning of the next 4 rows. Bind off the remaining 8 stitches.

Finishing
COLLAR

With A, pick up approximately 64 (68, 72, 76) stitches around neckline. Work in k1, p1 rib for 3" (7.5cm). Change to B and work in pattern for 2 rows more. Bind off.

Sew the shoulder seams. Set in the sleeves; sew side and sleeve seams. Weave in the ends. Block lightly to measurements.

RED TRIM (MAKE 2)

Using double-pointed needles and CC, cast on 4 stitches.

Work I-cord for 26" (66cm).

Bind off, weave in ends, and sew along the front edges of the cardigan with mattress stitch, being careful to hide the seams.

Sew in zipper using needle and thread. With a contrasting-colored thread, baste each side to the zipper, then unzip. With the matching thread, and using backstitch, sew the zipper in place, tucking the top ends of the zipper between the zipper and the garment. If necessary, whipstitch the edges of the zipper to the garment.

Rose Red Wrap

Every variation of the name Red in fairy tales conjures up an image of a plucky girl who has grand adventures despite trying to live a simple life. This shrug, inspired by the story of two sisters, a dwarf, and an enchanted bear, tries to be simple, too. Knit mostly flat, the sleeves are knit by casting on extra stitches, then later folding them over.

← DESIGNED BY JOAN OF DARK (A.K.A. TONI CARR) →

SKILL LEVEL

Intermediate

SIZES

S (M, L, XL)

FINISHED MEASUREMENTS

Back width at underarm: 20 (20¾, 21¾, 23½)" (51 [53, 55, 59.5]cm)

Back length from neck to point: 16 (17, 18½, 19¼)" (40.5 [43, 47, 49]cm)

MATERIALS

✦ Knit Picks Wool of the Andes (100% Peruvian highland wool, 1¾ oz/50g, 110 yd/100m): 4 (5, 6, 7) skeins in Garnet Heather

4 MEDIUM

✦ Size 9 (5mm) 29" circular needle, or size needed to obtain gauge

✦ Set of 5 size 9 (5mm) double-pointed needles, or size needed to obtain gauge

✦ Split-ring stitch marker

✦ Tapestry needle

GAUGE

18 stitches and 44 rows = 4" (10cm) in garter stitch

Fairy Facts

Children's book author Jon Scieszka has written stories with a slightly different twist on fairy tales we know and love.

Wrap

With circular needle, cast on 2 stitches. Knit 1 row.

Increase Row 1: Kfb, knit to end.

Place a marker to indicate the right side of the garment.

Repeat Increase Row 1 until there are 70 (74, 78, 86) stitches on the needle.

Knit 2 rows, work Increase Row 1 twice.

Repeat the last 4 rows until there are 90 (94, 98, 106) stitches on the needle.

Increase Row 2: [Kfb] twice, knit to end.

Repeat Increase Row 2 until there are 106 (110, 118, 126) stitches on the needle.

Sleeves

Next row: Cast on 19 (21, 21, 22) stitches, knit the cast-on stitches, knit to end.

Repeat the last row once more—144 (152, 160, 170) stitches.

Work even in garter stitch until sleeves measure 5½ (6, 7, 7)" (14 [15, 18, 18]cm) from sleeve cast-on, ending with a wrong-side row.

Neck

K57 (60, 63, 67), join a second ball of yarn, bind off the center 30 (32, 34, 36) stitches, knit to end—57 (60, 63, 67) stitches each side.

Work even in garter stitch on both sides until sleeves measure 10½ (11, 13½, 13½)" (26.5 [28, 34.5, 34.5] cm) from the sleeve cast-on, ending with a wrong-side row.

Shape Fronts

RIGHT FRONT

Rows 1, 3, and 5 (RS): K2tog, knit to end—54 (57, 60, 64) stitches after Row 5.

Rows 2, 4, and 6: Knit.

Row 7: Bind off 4 (4, 6, 6) stitches, knit to end—50 (53, 54, 58) stitches.

Row 8: Bind off 14 (16, 16, 17) stitches, knit to end—36 (37, 38, 41) stitches.

Row 9: Bind off 4 (4, 4, 6) stitches, knit to the end—32 (33, 34, 35) stitches.

Row 10: Bind off 4 stitches, knit to the end—28 (29, 30, 31) stitches.

Row 11: Bind off 5 (5, 6, 6) stitches, knit to end—23 (24, 24, 25) stitches.

Row 12: Bind off 4 stitches, knit to the end—19 (20, 20, 21) stitches.

Row 13: Bind off 6 (7, 7, 8) stitches, knit to end—13 stitches.

Row 14: Knit to the last 2 stitches, p2tog—12 stitches.

Row 15: K2tog, knit to end—11 stitches.

Rows 16–24: Repeat Rows 14 and 15—2 stitches after Row 24.

Bind off.

LEFT FRONT

Rows 1, 3, and 5 (RS): Knit to the last 2 stitches, ssk—54 (57, 60, 64) stitches after Row 5.

Rows 2, 4, and 6: Knit.

Rows 16–24: Repeat Rows 13 and 14—2 stitches after Row 24.

Bind off.

Finishing

Fold sleeves over and sew sleeve and side seams.

RIGHT FRONT TIE

With the right side facing, starting at the side seam and working to the front edge, pick up 28 (30, 30, 32) stitches.

Knit 4 rows.

Decrease Row: K1, k2tog, knit to the last 3 stitches, ssk, k1—2 stitches decreased.

Repeat Decrease Row every 9th row twice more, then every 5th row until 8 stitches remain.

Work even in garter stitch until tie measures 22" (56cm) from pick-up or to desired length.

Bind off.

LEFT FRONT TIE

Work same as Right Front Tie, starting at the lower front edge and working to the side seam.

SLEEVE BANDS (OPTIONAL)

With the right side facing, double-pointed needles, and starting at the seam, pick up 40 (44, 48, 48) stitches evenly around the sleeve opening.

Place marker and join to work in the round.

Work 4 rows in k2, p2 rib.

Bind off in pattern.

Weave in all ends and block lightly.

Row 7: Bind off 4 (4, 6, 6) stitches, knit to end—50 (53, 54, 58) stitches.

Row 8: Bind off 14 (16, 16, 17) stitches, knit to end—36 (37, 38, 41) stitches.

Row 9: Bind off 4 (4, 4, 6) stitches, knit to end—32 (33, 34, 35) stitches.

Row 10: Bind off 4 stitches, knit to end—28 (29, 30, 31) stitches.

Row 11: Bind off 5 (5, 6, 6) stitches, knit to end—23 (24, 24, 25) stitches.

Row 12: Bind off 4 stitches, knit to end—19 (20, 20, 21) stitches.

Row 13: Bind off 6 (7, 7, 8) stitches, knit to end—13 stitches.

Row 14: Knit to the last 2 stitches, ssk—12 stitches.

Row 15: K2tog, knit to end—11 stitches.

Bookish Belle Mitts

In Rilana's favorite movie adaptation of *Beauty and the Beast*, the beautiful heroine is lost in a world of books and ignores the provincial town life around her. These dainty fingerless mitts are designed for beautiful bookworms everywhere to keep their hands warm while they read their favorite stories.

←— DESIGNED BY RILANA RILEY-MUNSON —→

SKILL LEVEL

Intermediate

SIZE

One size

FINISHED MEASUREMENTS

7" (18cm) circumference x 8¾" (22cm) long

MATERIALS

+ Knit Picks Palette (100% Peruvian highland wool, 1¾ oz/50g, 231 yd/211m): 1 skein in Custard (MC) **(1)** SUPER FINE

+ Knit Picks Palette (100% Peruvian highland wool, 1¾ oz/50g, 231 yd/211m): 1 skein in Serrano (CC) **(1)** SUPER FINE

+ Size 2 (2.75mm) straight needles, or size needed to obtain gauge

+ Tapestry needle

+ 2 half-inch leaf buttons (optional)

GAUGE

32 stitches and 40 rows = 4" (10cm) in stockinette stitch

STITCH PATTERN

Rose Stems

Row 1 (RS): *K2, p4, k2tog, yo, k4; repeat from * to end.
Row 2: *P6, k4, p2; repeat from * to end.
Row 3: *K1, p4, k2tog, yo, k5; repeat from * to end.
Row 4: *P7, k4, p1; repeat from * to end.
Row 5: *P4, k2tog, yo, k6; repeat from * to end.
Row 6: *P8, k4; repeat from * to end.
Row 7: *K3, yo, ssk, p4, k3; repeat from * to end.
Row 8: *P3, k4, p5; repeat from * to end.
Row 9: *K4, yo, ssk, p4, k2; repeat from * to end.
Row 10: *P2, k4, p6; repeat from * to end.
Row 11: *K5, yo, ssk, p4, k1; repeat from * to end.
Row 12: *P1, k4, p7; repeat from * to end.
Repeat Rows 1–12 for pattern.

Mitts (make 2)

Using MC, cast on 96 stitches.

Row 1 (RS): Purl.

Row 2: Purl.

Work in stockinette stitch, beginning with a knit row, for 2" (5cm), ending with a wrong-side row.

Next row (RS): *K2tog; repeat from * to end—48 stitches.

Work in garter stitch for 1" (2.5cm), ending with a wrong-side row.

Next row (RS): K1, M1, [k4, M1] 5 times, k6, [M1, k4] 5 times, M1, k1—60 stitches.

Next row: Purl.

Work Rows 1–12 of Rose Stems pattern 5 times.

Work in k1, p1 rib for 4 rows. Bind off in pattern.

FINISHING

Fold the mitt in half lengthwise. Sew the side seam, leaving a 1¾" (4.5cm) opening for the thumb beginning 2" (5cm) down from top edge.

Roses (make 2)

Using CC, cast on 5 stitches.

Row 1 (RS): Knit.

Row 2: *K1, M1; repeat from * to last stitch, k1—9 stitches.

Row 3: Purl.

Row 4: *K1, M1; repeat from * to last stitch, K1—17 stitches.

Row 5: Purl.

Row 6: *K1, M1; repeat from * to last stitch, K1—33 stitches.

Row 7: Purl.

Row 8: *K1, M1; repeat from * to last stitch, K1—65 stitches.

Row 9: Purl.

Bind off.

Coil the piece into a rose shape and sew it to the mitts as shown. Weave in the ends. Optional: sew the leaf button at the base of the rose, opposite the side that corresponds with the hand of the glove (right side for left glove, left side for right glove).

What's in a Name?

The same fairy tales have often been retold in different countries and languages. Sometimes the title changes from variation to variation. Can you tell which modern fairy tale goes with its more exotic-sounding counterpart?

———————— • ————————

1. Sun, Moon, and Talia   a. Rapunzel
2. Le Petit Chaperon Rouge   b. Sleeping Beauty
3. Silverhair   c. Cinderella
4. Petrosinella   d. The Little Mermaid
5. Schneewittchen   e. Snow White
6. Aschenputtel   f. Little Red Riding Hood
7. Den Lille Havfrue   g. Goldilocks and the Three Bears
8. La Belle et la Bête   h. Beauty and the Beast

Answers: 1. b, 2. f, 3. g, 4. a, 5. e, 6. c, 7. d, 8. h

Fairest of Them All Top

Modern-day princesses can wear this dainty top with jeans and ballet flats, or pair it with the matching skirt (page 74) to create a girly, twirly dress with decorative ribbon. They'll love pretending to be their favorite fairy-tale heroine.

← DESIGNED BY ABIGAIL HORSFALL →

SKILL LEVEL

Intermediate

SIZES

2 (4, 6, 8, 10) years

FINISHED MEASUREMENTS

Bust: 17½ (19, 20¼, 21¾, 23¼)" (44.5 [48.5, 51, 55, 59]cm)

Length (without sleeves): 10 (10½, 12½, 14½, 15½)" (25.5 [26.5, 32, 37, 39.5]cm)

MATERIALS

✦ Three Irish Girls Springvale DK (100% superwash merino, 4 oz/113.5g, 270 yd/247m): 1 (1, 2, 2, 3) skeins in Paper Lanterns **3 LIGHT**

✦ Size 5 (3.75mm) 32" circular needle, or size needed to obtain gauge

✦ 2 stitch markers

✦ Tapestry needle

✦ 4 safety pins or locking stitch markers

✦ 2 yd (1.8m) elastic thread

✦ 1 yd (0.9m) coordinating ribbon, 1" (2.5cm) wide

GAUGE

22 stitches and 32 rows = 4" (10cm) in stockinette stitch

SPECIAL SKILLS

Short rows (page 139)

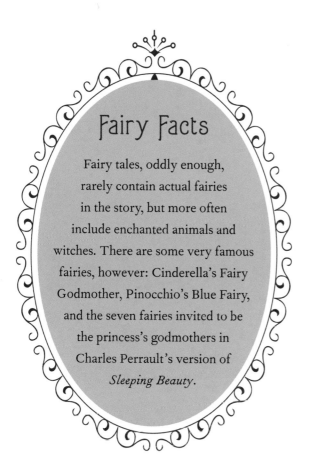

Fairy Facts

Fairy tales, oddly enough, rarely contain actual fairies in the story, but more often include enchanted animals and witches. There are some very famous fairies, however: Cinderella's Fairy Godmother, Pinocchio's Blue Fairy, and the seven fairies invited to be the princess's godmothers in Charles Perrault's version of *Sleeping Beauty*.

Bodice

Cast on 96 (104, 112, 120, 128) stitches, preferably using a stretchy cast-on, such as the German twisted cast-on technique.

Place marker and join for working in the round.

Round 1: *K2, p2; repeat from * around.

Round 2: Knit.

Round 3: *P2, k2; repeat from * around.

Round 4: Knit.

Repeat Rounds 1–4 until work measures 3½ (4, 4, 5, 5)" (9 [10, 10, 12.5, 12.5]cm) in length.

Purl 3 rounds.

Knit 3 rounds.

EYELET ROUND

Sizes 2 and 10 only: K3, k2tog, [yo] 3 times, *k6, k2tog, [yo] 3 times; repeat from * to the last 5 stitches, k3, k2tog, [yo] 3 times.

Size 4 only: *(K5, k2tog, [yo] 3 times, k6, k2tog, [yo] 3 times) 3 times, k5, k2tog, [yo] 3 times; repeat from * once more.

Size 6 only: *K6, k2tog, [yo] 3 times; repeat from * to end.

Size 8 only: *(K7, k2tog, [yo] 3 times, k6, k2tog, [yo] 3 times) 3 times, k7, k2tog, [yo] 3 times; repeat from * once more.

All sizes: Knit 3 rounds, working k1 once in the triple yo.

Purl 3 rounds.

Work in stockinette (knit every round) for 3½ (4, 5, 6, 7)" (9 [10, 12.5, 15, 18]cm) or until piece measures 1½ (1½, 2, 2, 2)" (3.8 [3.8, 5, 5, 5]cm) less than desired finished length.

Edging
SETUP ROUND

Sizes 2 and 8: Knit.

Sizes 4 and 10: K50 (62), k2tog, k50 (62), k2tog.

Size 6: K56, M1, k56, M1.

96 (102, 114, 120, 126) stitches remain.

Round 1: *K2tog, yo, k2, yo, ssk; repeat from * around.

Round 2: Knit.

Repeat these 2 rounds 4 (4, 6, 6, 6) times total, then repeat Round 1 once more.

Purl 2 rounds.

Bind off loosely knitwise.

Sleeves (make 2)

NOTES: Sleeves begin at the top (neck) edge.

After placement, slip markers as they are reached.

Cast on 42 (46, 46, 54, 54) stitches, preferably using a stretchy cast-on.

Row 1 (WS): P2, *k2, p2; repeat from * to end.

Row 2: Knit.

Row 3: K2, *p2, k2; repeat from * to end.

Row 4: Knit.

Row 5: P2, *k2, p2; repeat from * to end.

Row 6: K12 (13, 13, 15, 15), M1, pm, k1, M1, k16 (18, 18, 22, 22), M1, k1, pm, M1, k12 (13, 13, 15, 15)—46 (50, 50, 58, 58) stitches.

Row 7: K2, p2, k2, purl to the last 6 stitches, k2, p2, k2.

Row 8: Knit.

Row 9: P2, k2, purl to the last 4 stitches, k2, p2.

Row 10: Knit to the first marker, M1, sm, k1, M1, knit to 1 stitch before the second marker, M1, k1, sm, M1, knit to end—50 (54, 54, 62, 62) stitches.

Row 11: Repeat Row 7, removing markers as they are reached.

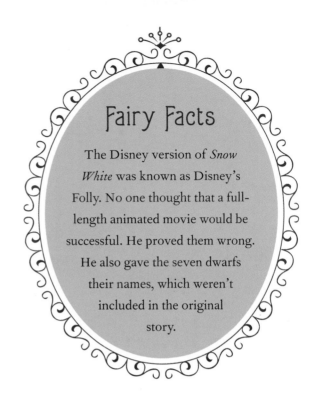

Fairy Facts

The Disney version of *Snow White* was known as Disney's Folly. No one thought that a full-length animated movie would be successful. He proved them wrong. He also gave the seven dwarfs their names, which weren't included in the original story.

SHAPE SHOULDERS WITH SHORT ROWS

Row 12 (all sizes): Knit to the last 7 stitches, wrap the next stitch, and turn work; purl to the last 7 stitches, wrap the next stitch, and turn work.

Knit to the last 11 stitches, wrap the next stitch, and turn work; purl to the last 11 stitches, wrap the next stitch, and turn work.

Knit to the last 15 stitches, wrap the next stitch, and turn work; purl to the last 15 stitches, wrap the next stitch, and turn work.

Knit to the last 19 stitches, wrap the next stitch, and turn work; purl to the last 19 stitches, wrap the next stitch, and turn work.

SIZES 4, 6, 8, AND 10:

Knit to the last 23 stitches, wrap the next stitch, and turn work; purl to the last 23 stitches, wrap the next stitch, and turn work.

SIZES 8 AND 10:

Knit to the last 27 stitches, wrap the next stitch, and turn work; purl to the last 27 stitches, wrap the next stitch, and turn work.

ALL SIZES:

Knit to end, lifting all wraps and knitting them together with their stitches.

Row 13: P2, k2, purl to the last 4 stitches, lifting all wraps and working them together with their stitches, k2, p2.

Row 14: *K1, M1; repeat from * to end.

Work in stockinette stitch for ½ (1, 1, 2, 2)" (1.3 [2.5, 2.5, 5, 5]cm) or until sleeve measures ½" (1.3cm) less than desired length, maintaining the 6-stitch border if desired.

Purl 3 rows.

Bind off loosely purlwise. This is the bottom edge of the sleeve.

Finishing

Weave in the ends and block the bodice and sleeves.

Lay the bodice flat, with the beginning of the round as a side seam. Place safety pins or locking stitch markers ½ (1, 1½, 1½, 2)" (1.3 [2.5, 3.8, 3.8, 5]cm) in from the sides on both the front and the back of the bodice. These pins will mark sleeve placement.

Using a separate 1 yd (0.9m) length of yarn for each seam, attach sleeves to the bodice as follows, preferably using whipstitch or mattress stitch, seaming only the top 1" (2.5cm) of the sleeve, leaving the rest to lie flat and drape over the shoulder:

Left side of Sleeve 1 to left front of Bodice.

Right side of Sleeve 1 to left back of Bodice.

Right side of Sleeve 2 to right front of Bodice.

Left side of Sleeve 2 to right back of Bodice.

Sew elastic thread into the first line of purl bumps on the wrong side of the top of each sleeve and pull to achieve desired fit before weaving in the elastic-thread ends securely. This will create slight gathers along the top of the sleeve and encourage ruffling in the sleeve cap. A looser sleeve will create more of an off-the-shoulder look while a tighter sleeve will create a squarer neckline.

Weave in the remaining ends. With a tapestry needle, thread the ribbon through the eyelets and tie it into a large bow.

A Little Princess Skirt

Every princess needs a skirt that twirls to her heart's content, like this circle skirt inspired by the heroine of Frances Hodgson Burnett's classic Edwardian novel *A Little Princess*. The construction is based on Elizabeth Zimmerman's Pi Shawl, and ruffles form as the stitches are doubled several times.

←→ DESIGNED BY TRISHA PAETCH ←→

SKILL LEVEL

Easy

SIZES

XS (S, M ,L, XL)

FINISHED MEASUREMENTS

Waistband: 22 (23, 24, 25, 25½)" (56 [58.5, 61, 63.5, 65]cm), adjustable with optional elastic

Length: 13 (15, 17, 19, 21)" (33 [38, 43, 48.5, 53.5]cm), without ribbon

MATERIALS

+ Three Irish Girls Springvale DK (100% superwash merino, 4 oz/113.5g, 270 yd/247m): 2 (3, 3, 4, 4) skeins in Paper Lanterns **(3) LIGHT**

+ 2 size 0 (2mm) 24" and/or 40" circular needles, or size needed to obtain gauge

+ Crochet hook

+ Scrap yarn

+ Stitch marker

+ 1" (2.5cm) wide elastic for the waistband

+ Matching thread and sewing needle

+ 2½ (2¾, 2¾, 3, 3) yd (2.3 [2.5, 2.5, 2.7, 2.7]m) of blue satin ribbon 2" (5cm) wide

+ Sewing machine

GAUGE

22 stitches and 30 rows = 4" (10cm) in stockinette stitch

SPECIAL SKILLS

Provisional cast-on (page 138)

Skirt

Provisionally cast on 121 (127, 132, 138, 140) stitches. Place marker and join to work in the round, being careful not to twist the stitches.

WAISTBAND CASING

Using the smaller needle, work in stockinette stitch for 1" (2.5cm).

Purl 1 round.

Work in stockinette stitch for 1" (2.5cm).

Undo the provisional cast-on and pick up 121 (127, 132, 138, 140) stitches with the second circular needle.

Cut the waistband elastic 1" (2.5cm) smaller than the actual waist measurement. Overlap the ends of the elastic by 1" (2.5cm) and stitch down with needle and thread to form a loop.

Fold the knitting at the purl ridge with the wrong sides together and insert the elastic between the knitted layers. Holding the 2 left-hand needles parallel (with picked-up stitches on the back needle) and working with the front right-hand needle, *knit 1 stitch from the front needle together with 1 stitch from the back needle; repeat from * around, enclosing the elastic to form the waistband.

Work in stockinette stitch until the skirt measures 3¼ (3¾, 4¼, 4¾, 5¼)" (8 [9.5, 11, 12, 13.5] cm) from the purl ridge.

Increase Round: *Kfb; repeat from * around—242 (254, 264, 276, 280) stitches.

Work in stockinette stitch for 6½ (7½, 8½, 9½, 10½)" (16.5 [19, 21.5, 24, 26.5]cm).

Repeat the Increase Round—484 (508, 528, 552, 560) stitches, switching to the larger needle when necessary.

Work in stockinette stitch for 3¼ (3¾, 4¼, 4¾, 5¼)" (8 [9.5, 11, 12, 13.5] cm).

Bind off.

Block lightly. Attach the ribbon along the bound-off edge using a zigzag stitch on the sewing machine, or hand sew. Seam the ends of the ribbon.

Cinderella Play Set

Serving three ungrateful women all day can really take a toll on a girl, and Cinderella is ready to dance the night away in a rockin' new party dress. Little girls will love this fairy-godmother-approved doll, a trio of mouse friends, and a pumpkin carriage to take them all to the ball.

↢ DESIGNED BY MARILEE NORRIS ↣

SKILL LEVEL

Intermediate

SIZE

One size

FINISHED MEASUREMENTS

Cinderella: 15" (38cm) tall

Pumpkin Carriage: 24" (61cm) in circumference

Mice: 4¼" (11cm) in circumference and 3¼" (8cm) long, excluding tail

MATERIALS

Cinderella

✦ Knit Picks Bare Fingering Sock Yarn (75% superwash merino wool, 25% nylon, 3½ oz/100g, 462 yd/422m): 1 skein in Natural (A) **1** SUPER FINE

✦ Knit Picks Chroma Fingering Sock Yarn (70% wool, 30% nylon, 3½ oz/100g, 396 yd/362m): 1 skein in Lollipop (B) **1** SUPER FINE

✦ Knit Picks Palette (100% Peruvian highland wool, 1¾ oz/50g, 231 yd/211m): 1 skein in Custard (C) **1** SUPER FINE

✦ DMC embroidery floss (100% polyester, 8¾ yd/8m): 2 hanks of E168 Silver (D)

✦ Small amount of pink embroidery floss

✦ 2 size 3 (3.25mm) circular needles, or size needed to obtain gauge

✦ Stitch markers

✦ 5mm craft eyes

✦ Polyester fiberfill

✦ Tapestry needle

✦ Embroidery needle

(continues)

Pumpkin Carriage

- Knit Picks Wool of the Andes Worsted (100% Peruvian highland wool, 1½oz/50g, 110 yd/100m): 2 skeins in Orange (MC) **(4) MEDIUM**

- Knit Picks Wool of the Andes Worsted (100% Peruvian highland wool, 1½ oz/50g, 110 yd/100m): 1 skein in Grass (CC) **(4) MEDIUM**

- Size 8 (5mm) circular needle, or size needed to obtain gauge

- Stitch marker

- Tapestry needle

- Stitch holders

- ½ yd (45.5cm) orange satin fabric

- Matching thread and sewing needle

- Sewing machine

- ½ yd (45.5cm) green grosgrain ribbon, 1" (2.5cm) wide

Mice

- Knit Picks Palette (100% Peruvian highland wool, 1½ oz/50g, 231 yd/211m): 1 skein in Asphalt Heather (A) **(1) SUPER FINE**

- Knit Picks Palette (100% Peruvian highland wool, 1½ oz/50g, 231 yd/211m): 1 skein in Marble Heather (B) **(1) SUPER FINE**

- Size 3 (3.25mm) circular knitting needle, or size needed to obtain gauge

- Stitch marker

- Polyester fiberfill

- Tapestry needle

- Small amounts of embroidery floss in pale pink, silver, purple, blue, and green

- Embroidery needle

- Small amount of ribbon, 1/8" (3mm) wide, in any color

GAUGE

Cinderella
28 stitches and 34 rows = 4" (10cm) in stockinette stitch using smaller needle

Pumpkin Carriage
20 stitches and 26 rows = 4" (10cm) in stockinette stitch

Mice
28 stitches and 36 rows = 4" (10cm) in stockinette stitch

SPECIAL SKILLS

3-needle bind-off (page 135)

I-cord (page 136)

Magic Loop (page 138)

Embroidery stitches (page 136)

NOTE

Unless otherwise instructed, all knitting is in the round using the Magic Loop method.

Fairy Facts

Cinderella's mice were her faithful companions in the movie adaptation by Disney. They kept her company, made her a dress, and helped her escape from the tower when Lady Tremaine locked her up to keep her from trying on the glass slipper.

Cinderella

HEAD AND BODY

With A and the smaller needle, cast on 40 stitches. Place marker and join to knit in the round.

Work in stockinette stitch until body measures 4" (10cm) from the cast-on edge.

Decrease Round 1: *[Ssk] twice, k12, [k2tog] twice; repeat from * to end—32 stitches.

Decrease Round 2: *Ssk, k12, k2tog; repeat from * to end—28 stitches.

Next round: Repeat Decrease Round 1—20 stitches.

Knit 1 round, placing a second marker after 10 stitches.

Next round: *Kfb, knit to 2 stitches before marker, kfb, k1; repeat from * to end.

Repeat last round until there are 48 stitches.

Knit 12 rounds.

Work Decrease Round 2 every round until there are 20 stitches.

Place craft eyes on Cinderella's head and attach following the manufacturer's instructions. Stuff the head with polyester fiberfill, and close the opening using the 3-needle bind-off. Stuff Cinderella's body, including her neck and shoulders, and sew the lower opening closed with tapestry needle and yarn. Weave in all the ends.

ARMS (MAKE 2)

With A and the smaller needle, cast on 10 stitches. Place marker and join to knit in the round.

Work in stockinette stitch until the arm measures 4½" (11.5cm). It is a good idea to stuff the arm lightly as you go.

Decrease Round: *K1, k2tog, k2; repeat from * to end.

Knit 1 round.

Increase Round: *K1, kfb, k2; repeat from * to end. Knit 7 rounds.

Stuff the hand with a small amount of fiberfill. Break yarn, leaving a 6" (15cm) tail. Thread the tail through the remaining stitches, pull tight, and secure.

LEGS (MAKE 2)

With A and the smaller needle, cast on 10 stitches. Place marker and join to knit in the round.

Work in stockinette stitch until the leg measures 6" (15cm). It is a good idea to stuff the leg lightly as you go.

Decrease Round: *K1, k2tog, k2; repeat from * to the end.

Knit 1 round.

Increase Round: *K1, kfb, k2; repeat from * to end.

Knit 11 rounds.

Stuff the foot with a small amount of fiberfill. Break yarn, leaving a 6" (15cm) tail. Thread the tail through the remaining stitches, pull tight, and secure.

Dress

FIRST RUFFLE

With B and the larger needle, cast on 80 stitches. Place marker and join to knit in the round.

Round 1: Knit.

Round 2: *K1, p1; repeat from * around.

Round 3: *P1, k1; repeat from * around.

Repeat Rounds 2 and 3 until ruffle measures 2½" (6.5cm) from cast-on edge.

Work in stockinette stitch for 1½" (3.8cm).

Decrease Round: *K2tog; repeat from * around—40 stitches.

Change to the smaller needle and knit 1 round. Break yarn and set aside.

SECOND RUFFLE

Work the same as the First Ruffle until it measures 2½" (6.5cm) from cast-on edge, then work the Decrease Round.

With the right sides of both ruffles facing you, place the second ruffle on top of the first ruffle so both sets of needles are aligned. The first ruffle should be peeking out from the bottom of the second ruffle. Using the second smaller needle, join the two ruffles by *knitting the first stitch of the second ruffle together with the first stitch of the first ruffle; repeat from * around.

BODICE

Continue with the smaller needle.

Decrease Round 1: *K2tog, k8; repeat from * around—36 stitches.

Decrease Round 2: *K2tog, k7; repeat from * around—4 stitches decreased.

Work in stockinette stitch for 2" (5cm).

Next round: *K1, p1; repeat from * around.

Next round: *P1, k1; repeat from * around.

Repeat the last 2 rounds once more.

Bind off in pattern. Break yarn, weave in all ends.

Tiara

NOTE: The tiara is knit flat from end to end. *Use all six strands at once.*

With D and the smaller needle, cast on 12 stitches.

Row 1: Bind off 10 stitches, k1, cast on 2 stitches at the end of the row—4 stitches.

Row 2: Sl 1, k3.

Row 3 (arch): Sl 1, k3; cast on 7 stitches at the end of the row—11 stitches.

Row 4: Bind off 7 stitches, knit to the end of the row—4 stitches.

Rows 5–9: Repeat Row 2.

Row 10: Insert the tip of the right-hand needle into a loop at the very tip of the tiara's arch, knit the first stitch on the left-hand needle, then lift the arch loop over the just-made stitch, k3.

Rows 11 and 12, 21 and 22: Repeat Row 2.

Rows 13–20, 23–30: Repeat Rows 3–10.

Row 31: Repeat Row 2.

Bind off 2 stitches, slip the stitch on the right-hand needle to the left-hand needle, then cast on 10 stitches—12 stitches.

Bind off. Cut embroidery floss, leaving a tail to secure the tiara onto Cinderella's head.

Slippers (make 2)

NOTE: Cinderella's slippers are knitted flat, then seamed to create the slipper shape. *Use all six strands at once.*

With D and the smaller needle, cast on 5 stitches, leaving a long tail for seaming.

Row 1: *Kfb; repeat from * to end—10 stitches.

Rows 2-16: Knit.

Row 17: *K2tog; repeat from * to end—5 stitches.

Cut embroidery floss, and draw it through the remaining stitches using a tapestry needle. Fold the slipper lengthwise, and seam it two-thirds of the way closed. This forms the toe of the slipper.

At the heel, sew 2 stitches to bring the edges together, then weave in the ends.

Finishing

Sew on Cinderella's arms and legs.

Cut several strands of C 20" (51cm) long for Cinderella's hair. Using a tapestry needle, secure the yarn under each knit stitch (both sides of the "V") along where the hairline would be. A natural place to start the hairline is right in front of the ridge that is created when you cast off. Tie the yarn in a knot. Create a second row of hair, directly behind the first row of hair, along the top ridge of the head. Next, you will place three more rows of hair horizontally across the back of her head, spaced so the bottom row is about one-third of the way down her head. Place the hair every other stitch. These last three rows help to create the illusion of a full head of hair.

Trim her hair slightly to even up the ends.

Take a small section of the front of her hair where her bangs would be. To create her bangs, swoop this hair to the side and around the back of her head. Secure it in place by tying it together with a few strands of hair from the back of her head.

Embroider Cinderella's mouth with some pink embroidery floss in a small V shape. Sew on her tiara, hiding the ends of it underneath her hair.

Last, dress that princess up in her party dress and put her glass slippers on her feet. It's time to find her happily ever after!

Pumpkin Carriage

With MC, cast on 32 stitches, leaving a long tail for seaming. Place marker and join to knit in the round, dividing stitches evenly for the Magic Loop method.

Round 1: *[Kfb] 3 times, p1; repeat from * around—56 stitches.

Round 2: *K6, p1; repeat from * around.

Round 3: *K1, [kfb] 4 times, k1, p1; repeat from * around—88 stitches.

Round 4: *K10, p1; repeat from * around.

Round 5: *[Kfb] 10 times, p1; repeat from * around—168 stitches.

Round 6: *K20, p1; repeat from * around.

Repeat Round 6 until piece measures 7" (18cm) from cast-on edge.

Decrease Round 1: *P2tog; repeat from * around—84 stitches.

Decrease Round 2: *K2tog; repeat from * around—42 stitches.

Eyelet Round: *K1, k2tog, [yo] twice; repeat from * around—56 stitches.

Decrease Round 3: *K2, k1 dropping the second yo; repeat from * around—42 stitches.

Knit 1 round.

Purl 1 round.

Knit 3 rounds.

Work picot bind-off as follows:

*Cast on 2 stitches, bind off 4 stitches, slip the stitch on the right-hand needle back to the left-hand needle; repeat from * around. Break yarn.

To close the hole in the bottom of the bag, turn the bag inside out. With a tapestry needle, weave the yarn end through the cast-on stitches in a long running stitch. Gently pull the yarn tight until the hole is closed. Weave in all ends.

PUMPKIN VINES (MAKE 3)

With CC, cast on 18 stitches loosely.

Row 1: *Kfb; repeat from * to end—36 stitches. Bind off all stitches purlwise.

PUMPKIN LEAF STEM (MAKE 1)

With CC, cast on 3 stitches. Work in I-cord for 1" (2.5cm). Cut yarn, and place stitches on holder. Set aside.

PUMPKIN LEAF (MAKE 1)

With CC, cast on 4 stitches.

Row 1: Sl 1, [kfb] twice, k1—6 stitches.

Row 2: Sl 1, knit to end.

Row 3: Sl 1, kfb, k2, kfb, k1—8 stitches.

Row 4: Repeat Row 2.

Break yarn, and place stitches on holder. Set aside.

Start another section of a Pumpkin Leaf as before and work through Row 4. *Do not break yarn.* Place stitches on holder. Set aside.

Place the stitches of the first leaf section onto the needle with the working yarn on the right, the 3 stitches of the stem, then the second leaf section with the working yarn on the right—19 stitches.

Rows 5–8: Repeat Row 2.

Row 9: Sl 1, ssk, knit to last 3 stitches, k2tog, k1.

Row 10: Repeat Row 2.

Repeat Rows 9 and 10 until 5 stitches remain.

Last row: Sl 1, k3tog, k1—3 stitches.

Bind off. Break yarn, and weave in all ends except for the tail on the end of the stem, which can be used for attaching the leaf to the pumpkin later.

Finishing

Sew the Pumpkin Leaf and Vines as desired around the upper edge of the pumpkin, just under the row of eyelets.

Lining the Pumpkin

Measure the circumference of the pumpkin and add 1" (2.5cm). This measurement will equal the length of the lining to be cut.

Measure the height of the pumpkin and double it. This measurement will equal the height of the lining to be cut.

Cut the lining according to the measurements you have taken. It will look like a long rectangle.

Fold the rectangle in half with the right sides together, and sew along the short edge with a ¼" (6mm) seam allowance. You now have a tube.

To create the bottom of the lining, with right sides together, sew a long running stitch through both layers of an open edge. Pull on the thread, gathering the material together as tightly as possible. Secure in place with a knot.

With the right sides of the fabric still together, fold down the top edge of the lining to the wrong side. You'll want the lining to be a couple inches taller than the actual height of the bag. It's a good idea to place the lining in the bag temporarily to check that you've got approximately the right height.

Sew a running stitch through the top edge of the lining. Place the lining back in the bag, and slowly pull on the thread to gather the material together.

Keep gathering the material until it is the same size as the opening of the bag. Make sure the gathers are even around the top of the lining, and secure them in place with a knot.

Pin the lining in place to the top of the bag just under the row of eyelets, and sew it in place.

Weave the green ribbon through the eyelets and tie the ends together in a knot. When pulled, it acts as a drawstring to close the bag.

Voilà! Cinderella now has transportation!

Mice

NOTE: The mice are knitted seamlessly in the round using the Magic Loop method. It's important to stuff your mice with fiberfill as you go before you seam them shut.

MOUSE 1

Body

With A, cast on 4 stitches. Place marker and join to knit in the round.

Round 1: *Kfb; repeat from * around—8 stitches.

Rounds 2 and 3: *Kfb, k1; repeat from * around—18 stitches after Round 3.

Round 4: *Kfb, k2; repeat from * around—24 stitches.

Round 5: *Kfb, k3; repeat from * around—30 stitches.

Rounds 6–13: Knit.

Round 14: *K2tog, k3; repeat from * around—24 stitches.

Rounds 15–17: Knit.

Round 18: *K2tog, k2; repeat from * around—18 stitches.

Rounds 19–23: Knit.

Round 24: *K2tog, k1; repeat from * around—12 stitches.

Rounds 25-28: Knit.

Round 29: *K2tog; repeat from * around—6 stitches.

Break yarn, thread it through the live stitches, and weave in all the ends.

Ears (make 2)

NOTE: The ears are knitted from the top down.

With A, cast on 8 stitches. Place marker and join to knit in the round.

Round 1: *Kfb, k1; repeat from * around—12 stitches.

Round 2: Knit.

Round 3: *Kfb, k2; repeat from * around—16 stitches.

Rounds 4–7: Knit.

Round 8: *K2tog, k2; repeat from * around—12 stitches.

Round 9: Knit.

Break yarn, leaving a long tail for sewing the ears to the mouse, and thread it through live stitches using a tapestry needle. Weave in the end at the top of the ear.

Tail

With A, cut 6 strands of yarn 12" (30.5cm) long, and using a tapestry needle, draw them through a couple of stitches on the mouse's bottom. Divide the yarn evenly into three sections, and braid the tail to the desired length. Place a knot in the end and trim.

MOUSE 2

Follow knitting instructions for Mouse 1, using yarn B for the Body, yarn A for the Ears, and both yarns A and B for the Tail.

MOUSE 3

Follow knitting instructions for Mouse 1 starting with yarn A and alternating it every 2 rounds with yarn B to create the stripes (knit the last 3 rounds in yarn B). Use yarn A for the Ears and Tail.

FINISHING

Sew the Ears onto each mouse's Body.

NOTE: When using the embroidery floss, use all six strands at once.

For all mice: Using light pink floss, embroider the nose using a satin stitch (page 136).

Mouse 1: Using a long running stitch and silver floss, embroider whiskers on each side of the mouse's face. Embroider French knots (page 136) for the eyes with purple floss. Using the ⅛" (3mm) wide ribbon, tie a tiny bow around one of the ears.

Mouse 2: Using a long running stitch and silver floss, embroider whiskers on each side of the mouse's face. Embroider French knots for the eyes with blue floss.

Mouse 3: Using a long running stitch and silver floss, embroider whiskers on each side of the mouse's face. Embroider French knots for the eyes with green floss.

Proper Princess Topper

This fancy party hat is sure to delight a birthday girl or add extra sparkle to a princess costume. Made with beaded silk and metallic yarns, this heirloom piece was inspired by a Halloween costume that Trisha's mother made from one of her grandmother's ball gowns.

←— DESIGNED BY TRISHA PAETSCH —→

SKILL LEVEL

Intermediate

SIZE

One size

FINISHED MEASUREMENTS

Circumference: 12" (30.5cm)

Height: 12" (30.5cm)

NOTE

This hat is intended to sit atop the head rather than around it.

MATERIALS

+ Tilli Tomas Beaded Plie (100% silk with beads, 3½ oz/100g, 140 yd/128m): 1 skein in Romance (A) **(3) LIGHT**

+ Habu Textiles N-69 (67% bamboo, 33% metallic, ½ oz /14g, 311 yd/284m): 1 cone in 20/1 Copper Bamboo (B) **(0) LACE**

+ Size US 0 (2mm) circular needle or double-pointed needles, or size needed to obtain gauge

+ Scrap yarn for provisional cast-on

+ 4mm crochet hook for provisional cast-on

+ Cable needle

+ Tapestry needle

+ Stitch markers

+ Pencil and paper

+ Paper-cutting scissors

+ Cellophane tape

+ 2 pieces of flexible needlepoint canvas, approximately 10.5" x 13.5" (26.5cm x 34.5cm)

+ ½ yd (45.5cm) round elastic cording in silver

GAUGE

22 stitches and 38 rows = 4" (10cm) in stockinette stitch

SPECIAL SKILLS

Provisional cast-on (page 138)

Cables (page 135)

Kitchener stitch (page 137)

SPECIAL INSTRUCTIONS

FC: Slip 3 stitches to cable needle and hold in front, k3, then k3 from cable needle.

Sl 1 wyif: Slip 1 stitch as if to purl with yarn in front.

SBC: Slip 1 stitch to cable needle and hold in back, k1 tbl, then p1 from cable needle.

SFC: Slip 1 stitch to cable needle and hold in front, p1, then k1 tbl from cable needle.

STITCH PATTERN

Cable Pattern (worked over 18 stitches)
Row 1 (RS): P4, SBC, k6, SFC, p3, k1.
Row 2: Sl 1 wyif, k3, p6, k4.
Row 3: P3, SBC, p1, k6, p1, SFC, p2, k1.
Row 4: Sl 1 wyif, k2, p2, k1, p6, k1, p2, k3.
Row 5: P2, SBC, p2, FC, p2, SFC, p1, k1.
Row 6: Sl 1 wyif, k1, p2, k2, p6, k2, p2, k2.
Row 7: P1, SBC, p3, k6, p3, SFC, k1.
Rows 8 and 10: Sl 1 wyif, p2, k3, p6, k3, p2, k1.
Row 9: P1, SFC, p3, k6, p3, SBC, k1.
Row 11: P2, SFC, p2, FC, p2, SBC, p1, k1.
Row 12: Sl 1 wyif, k1, p2, k2, p6, k2, p2, k2.
Row 13: P3, SFC, p1, k6, p1, SBC, p2, k1.
Row 14: Sl 1 wyif, k2, p2, k1, p6, k1, p2, k3.
Row 15: P4, SFC, k6, SBC, p3, k1.
Row 16: Sl 1 wyif, k3, p10, k4.
Repeat Rows 1–16 for pattern.

Hat

Use scrap yarn and a crochet hook to provisionally cast on 18 stitches. Leaving a 12" (30.5cm) tail, hold both yarns together and work Row 1 of the Cable Pattern into the provisional cast-on. Work Rows 1–16 of the Cable Pattern twice, then Rows 1–15 once more. Piece should measure approximately 12" (30.5cm). Do not cut the yarn.

Undo the provisional cast-on, picking up the stitches as you go, and graft the two ends together using Kitchener stitch and the yarn tail.

With the right sides facing and both yarns held together, pick up and knit 60 stitches in the slipped stitches along the edge of the band. Place marker and join to work in the round. Place a marker after every 15th stitch while working the first round.

Rounds 1–5: Knit.

Round 6: *Knit to 2 stitches before the marker, k2tog, sm; repeat from * around.

Repeat Rounds 1–6 until 4 stitches remain. Cut the yarn, thread it through the 4 stitches, and secure.

Veil

With B, cast on 68 stitches. Work in garter stitch for 12" (30.5cm) or to desired length.

SHAPING

Row 1: *K2tog; repeat from * to end—34 stitches.

Rows 2 and 4: Knit.

Row 3: Repeat Row 1—17 stitches.

Bind off. Sew the shaped end of the veil to the top of the hat. Weave in all ends. Wet block, being careful not to crush the veil, and lay it flat to dry.

Finishing

Trace the finished hat onto a large piece of paper. Move the hat so that the right-hand edge of the fabric exactly meets the left-hand edge of the tracing, and trace again. Move the hat so that the left-hand edge of the fabric exactly meets the right-hand edge of the first tracing, and trace again.

You now have a shape that resembles about a third of a circle. Cut on the outside tracing lines, and roll the paper to form a cone. Tape the edges in place, and fit the paper cone inside the hat, trimming any excess that is in the way. Trim around the lower edge so that the paper cone is ½" (13mm) shorter than the hat.

Remove the tape and use the paper cone as a template to trace the shape onto the needlepoint plastic canvas. (You will need to use two pieces of canvas seamed together.) Cut the plastic canvas on the tracing lines, overlap the side edges slightly, and use scrap yarn to seam them securely.

Insert the plastic cone into the hat, and sew the lower edge of the plastic to the inside of the hat, preferably with an overcast stitch and matching sewing thread.

Tie the elastic cording securely to the plastic canvas about 1" (2.5cm) up on the inside of the hat. Lay the hat flat with the cording at one edge to easily find the opposite point at which to attach the other end of the elastic. Thread the elastic through the canvas here and secure the end as before by tying it to the plastic canvas after the hat has been placed on the royal head and the elastic adjusted to ensure the best fit. Trim any excess cording.

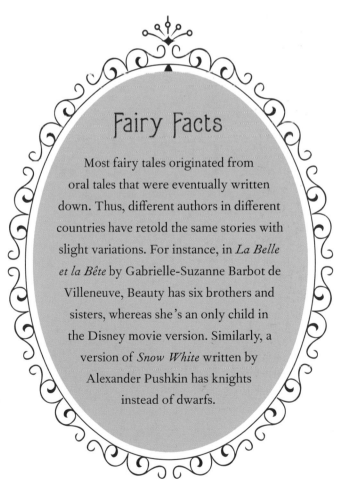

Fairy Facts

Most fairy tales originated from oral tales that were eventually written down. Thus, different authors in different countries have retold the same stories with slight variations. For instance, in *La Belle et la Bête* by Gabrielle-Suzanne Barbot de Villeneuve, Beauty has six brothers and sisters, whereas she's an only child in the Disney movie version. Similarly, a version of *Snow White* written by Alexander Pushkin has knights instead of dwarfs.

Something Wicked

vil. Malicious. Cruel. Every good fairy tale has an even better villain. In modern fairy tales, we're often just as interested in the villain's backstory as we are in the hero's inevitable triumph. And why not? These bad boys and femme fatales demand only the best—eternal youth, a royal couple's firstborn, a candy cottage—and their sense of fashion is equally extravagant.

The designs in this chapter pay tribute to these dark, yet glamorous, mischief makers with rich embellishments and fancy colorwork. From an infinity scarf that could be made from Rumpelstiltskin's spun gold to a gorgeous beret fit for the Queen of Hearts, let these projects unleash your wicked side. A black lace shawl, poison-green shrug, and sumptuous vest fit for a Snow Queen showcase the glam style of these dark forces, while playful gingerbread mitts, a stuffed dragon, and tongue-in-cheek pot holder prove that being sinister doesn't mean you can't have a sense of humor, too.

Maleficence

Fairy-tale villains aren't all ugly witches or trolls. On the contrary, some of our favorite evildoers are beautiful enchantresses and wicked queens. One of the most iconic antagonists is the sorceress from Walt Disney's *Sleeping Beauty,* who puts a curse on the newborn Aurora—all while looking fabulous—and this lace shrug pays homage to her sinful allure.

← DESIGNED BY TANIS GRAY →

SKILL LEVEL

Intermediate

SIZE

One size fits many

FINISHED MEASUREMENTS

32" (81cm) long x 18" (45.5cm) wide, after blocking and before seaming

MATERIALS

✦ Neighborhood Fiber Company Studio Worsted (100% merino wool, 8 oz/226g, 400 yd/366m): 1 skein in Clintonville

(4) MEDIUM

✦ Size 8 (5mm) 24" circular needle, or size needed to obtain gauge

✦ Tapestry needle

GAUGE

16 stitches and 20 rows = 4" (10cm) in rib pattern, after blocking

16 stitches and 18 rows = 4" (10cm) in Lace pattern, after blocking

STITCH PATTERN

Lace

Row 1 (RS): K1, *k1, yo, ssk, yo, k2tog, k3, ssk, yo, k2tog, yo, k2; repeat from * to the last stitch, k1.

Row 2 and all WS rows: K1, purl to the last stitch, k1.

Row 3: K1, *k2, yo, ssk, yo, k2tog, k1, ssk, yo, k2tog, yo, k3; repeat from * to the last stitch, k1.

Row 5: K1, *k3, yo, ssk, yo, sk2p, yo, k2tog, yo, k4; repeat from * to the last stitch, k1.

Row 7: K1, *k4, yo, ssk, k1, k2tog, yo, k5; repeat from * to the last stitch, k1.

Row 9: K1, *k5, yo, sk2p, yo, k6; repeat from * to the last stitch, k1.

Row 11: K1, *k4, k2tog, yo, k1, yo, ssk, k5; repeat from * to the last stitch, k1.

Row 13: K1, *k3, k2tog, yo, k3, yo, ssk, k4; repeat from * to the last stitch, k1.

Row 15: K1, *k2, k2tog, yo, k1, yo, sk2p, yo, k1, yo, ssk, k3; repeat from * to the last stitch, k1.

Row 17: K1, *k1, k2tog, yo, ssk, yo, k3, yo, k2tog, yo, ssk, k2; repeat from * to the last stitch, k1.

Row 19: K1, *k2tog, yo, ssk, yo, k5, yo, k2tog, yo, ssk, k1; repeat from * to the last stitch, k1.

Rows 21, 23, 25, and 27: Knit.

Repeat Rows 1–28 for pattern.

Fairy Facts

In "The Wild Swans," fairies gather nettles in graveyards and the heroine, Elisa, knits them into shirts that will help her brothers.

Shrug

Cast on 68 stitches. Work in k2, p2 rib for 15 rows.

Next row (WS): Purl, increasing 4 stitches evenly across—72 stitches.

Work Rows 1–28 of Lace pattern 4 times.

Next row (RS): Knit, decreasing 4 stitches evenly across—68 stitches.

Work in k2, p2 rib for 15 rows. Bind off in pattern.

Finishing

Block to measurements. Fold the shrug in half lengthwise. Seam the long edges 5" (12.5cm) in from the ends on each side, or as desired. Weave in the ends.

Good Versus Evil

In most fairy tales, good wins over evil and the wicked get their just deserts.

How does each villain get defeated?

1. Is shoved into an oven and cooked
2. Is forced to wear red-hot iron shoes and dance until he/she dies
3. Is cut open and filled with stones
4. Eyes are poked out by birds
5. Melts after water is thrown on him/her
6. Tears him/herself in two
7. Is struck down by a bear

a. The Wicked Witch of the West
b. Cinderella's stepsisters
c. The Big Bad Wolf
d. Snow White's Wicked Queen
e. Rumpelstiltskin
f. The Witch in *Hansel and Gretel*
g. The evil dwarf in *Snow White and Rose Red*

Answers: 1. f, 2. d, 3. c, 4. b, 5. a, 6. e, 7. g

Raven Shawlette

The raven is often considered a bird of ill will, bad omens, death, and a forewarning of war. The Brothers Grimm retell multiple fairy tales involving ravens that show how superstitious people act toward the birds. In fact, ravens are enigmatic, playful tricksters and highly intelligent. This triangular shawlette celebrates these misunderstood black beauties.

DESIGNED BY RILANA RILEY-MUNSON

SKILL LEVEL

Intermediate

SIZE

One size

FINISHED MEASUREMENTS

50" (127cm) wide x 20" (51cm) long, after blocking

MATERIALS

✦ Patons Grace (100% mercerized cotton, 1¾ oz/50g, 136 yd/124m): 3 skeins in 62040 Night (3) LIGHT

✦ Size 6 (4mm) 24" circular needle, or size needed to obtain gauge

✦ Stitch markers

✦ Tapestry needle

GAUGE

24 stitches and 32 rows = 4" (10cm) in stockinette stitch

SPECIAL INSTRUCTIONS

Sk2p: Slip 1 stitch purlwise, knit 2 stitches together, pass the slipped stitch over and off the needle—2 stitches decreased.

NOTES

Charts are read from right to left.

The full charts are knitted on both sides of the center markers, mirrored.

The wrong-side rows are not included in the charts and should be worked as Row 2.

Shawl

Cast on 5 stitches.

Knit 4 rows.

Row 1 (RS): K2, yo, k1, yo, k2—7 stitches.

Row 2: K2, purl to the last 2 stitches, k2.

Row 3: K2, pm, yo, k1, yo, pm, k1 (center stitch), pm, yo, k1, yo, pm, k2—11 stitches.

Row 4: Repeat Row 2.

Row 5: K2, sm, yo, knit to next marker, yo, sm, k1 (center stitch), sm, yo, knit to the last marker, yo, sm, k2—15 stitches.

Row 6: Repeat Row 2.

Repeat Rows 5 and 6 until there are 73 stitches in each stockinette stitch section between markers—151 stitches total.

Work Chart A 3 times (or more, if desired, for a longer shawl).

Work Chart B once.

Bind off loosely.

Finishing

Weave in the ends. Block.

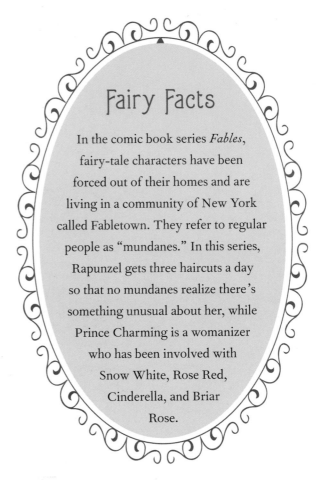

Fairy Facts

In the comic book series *Fables*, fairy-tale characters have been forced out of their homes and are living in a community of New York called Fabletown. They refer to regular people as "mundanes." In this series, Rapunzel gets three haircuts a day so that no mundanes realize there's something unusual about her, while Prince Charming is a womanizer who has been involved with Snow White, Rose Red, Cinderella, and Briar Rose.

Stitch Key

☐ Knit

⊡ Yo

⧄ SK2P

☐ Repeat

Chart A

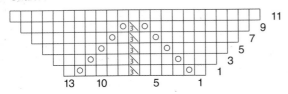

Note: Charts show right side rows only. Purl wrong side rows.

Chart B

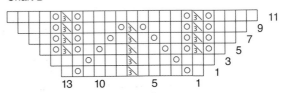

Dark Dream Socks

A shimmering moon casts long shadows across the Enchanted Forest.
A cloaked figure slinks through the trees, pausing to check if anyone is
following. Nefarious characters will delight in the spooky atmosphere these
socks evoke, knowing that wicked schemes are afoot.

⟵— DESIGNED BY LAURA HOHMAN —⟶

SKILL LEVEL

Experienced

SIZES

S (M, L)

FINISHED MEASUREMENTS

6½ (8, 9)" (16.5 [20.5, 23]cm) foot
circumference

MATERIALS

✦ Knit Picks Stroll Sock Yarn
(75% superwash merino wool,
25% nylon, 1¾ oz/50g,
231 yd/211.2m): 1 (2, 2) skeins in
Black (A) **1** SUPER FINE

✦ Knit Picks Stroll Sock Yarn
(75% superwash merino wool,
25% nylon, 1¾ oz/50g,
231 yd/211.2m): 1 (1, 1) skeins in
Dusk (B) **1** SUPER FINE

✦ Knit Picks Stroll Glimmer Yarn
(70% fine superwash merino
wool, 25% nylon, 5% Stellina,
1¾ oz/50g, 231yd/211.2m):
1 skein in White (C)
1 SUPER FINE

✦ Set of 5 size 1 (2.25mm) double-
pointed needles

✦ Set of 5 size 2 (3mm) double-
pointed needles, or size
needed to obtain gauge

✦ Stitch marker

✦ Tapestry needle

GAUGE

8 stitches and 40 rows = 1" (2.5cm)
in stockinette stitch using larger
needles

SPECIAL SKILLS

Stranded knitting (page 139)

Kitchener stitch (page 137)

Duplicate stitch (page 136)

Cuff

With smaller needles and A, cast on 56 (64, 72) stitches.

Place marker and join into a round, being careful not to twist stitches.

Work in Twisted Rib as follows:

Rounds 1-4: *K2, p2; repeat from * around.

Round 5: *K2tog leaving both stitches on the left-hand needle, knit into the back of the first stitch and drop both stitches from the needle, p2; repeat from * around.

Repeat Rounds 1–4 for 1 (1½, 2)" (2.5 [3.8, 5]cm).

Body

Change to larger needles and work 39 rounds in chart pattern, working moon in B.

Heel

With A, k14 (16, 18) and slip 14 (16, 18) stitches from the previous needle onto same needle—28 (32, 36) stitches for heel.

Divide the remaining (instep) stitches onto 2 needles.

Work heel back and forth as follows:

Row 1 (WS): Sl 1, purl to end.

Row 2: *Sl 1, k1; repeat from * to end.

Repeat Rows 1 and 2 until heel measures 2 (2½, 3)" (5 [6.5, 7.5]cm), approximately 24 (28, 32) rows.

TURN HEEL

Row 1: Sl 1, p15 (17, 19), p2tog, p1, turn.

Row 2: Sl 1, k5, ssk, k1, turn.

Row 3: Sl 1, purl to 1 stitch before the gap, p2tog, p1, turn.

Row 4: Sl 1, knit to 1 stitch before the gap, ssk, k1, turn.

Repeat Rows 3 and 4 until all heel stitches have been worked—16 (18, 20) stitches.

With a spare needle, pick up and k15 (17, 19) stitches along the side of the heel flap.

With a second needle, k28 (32, 36) instep stitches.

With a third needle, pick up and k15 (17, 19) stitches along the other side of the heel flap, k8 (9, 10) heel stitches.

Slip the remaining 8 (9, 10) heel stitches onto the end of the first needle—74 (84, 94) stitches.

GUSSETS

Decrease Round

Needle 1: Knit to the last 3 stitches, ssk, k1.

Needle 2: Work in Twisted Rib (see cuff instructions).

Needle 3: K1, k2tog, knit to end.

Continue in pattern as established, working Decrease Round every other round until there are 56 (64, 72) stitches.

Continue even in pattern until foot measures 2" (5cm) less than desired length.

TOE

Decrease Round

Needle 1: Knit to the last 3 stitches, k2tog, k1.

Needle 2: K1, ssk, work in Twisted Rib to the last 3 stitches, k2tog, k1.

Dark Dreams Pattern

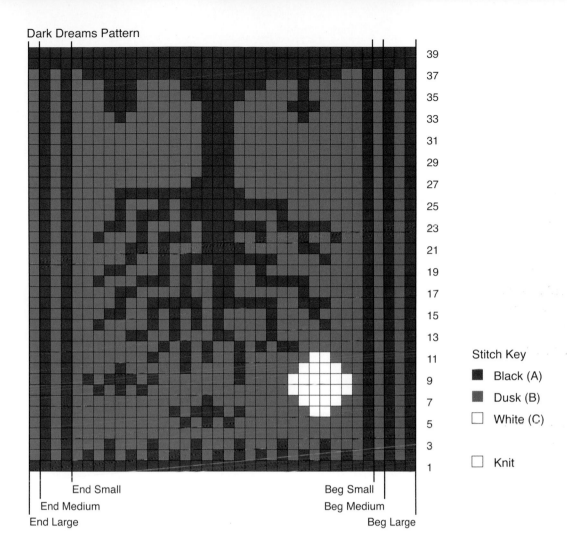

39
37
35
33
31
29
27
25
23
21
19
17
15
13
11
9
7
5
3
1

End Small
End Medium
End Large

Beg Small
Beg Medium
Beg Large

Stitch Key

■ Black (A)

■ Dusk (B)

□ White (C)

□ Knit

Needle 3: K1, ssk, knit to end.

Even Round

Needle 1: Knit.

Needle 2: K3, work in Twisted Rib to the last 3 stitches, k3.

Needle 3: Knit.

Repeat the last 2 rounds until 16 (20, 20) stitches remain.

With Needle 3, k4 (5, 5) from Needle 1—8 (10, 10) stitches on each needle.

Cut yarn, leaving a 12" (30.5cm) tail. Thread it onto tapestry needle and graft the stitches together using Kitchener stitch.

Use tapestry needle to pull the tail through the end of the sock.

FINISHING

Using duplicate stitch, add moon where indicated on chart.

Weave in all yarn ends. Soak socks and block to relax color knitting.

Candy Witch Fingerless Gloves

You might mistake these wristlets for actual gingerbread—they look good enough to eat! Modern witches might not live in candy-covered houses, but they can wear temptations on their hands to lure admirers and compliments. Customize the bobble gumdrops to suit your favorite flavors.

⟵ **DESIGNED BY LAURA HOHMAN** ⟶

SKILL LEVEL

Intermediate

SIZES

S (M, L, XL)

FINISHED MEASUREMENTS

Finished palm circumference: 6 (6¾, 8, 9)" (15 [17, 20.5, 23]cm)

MATERIALS

✦ Knit Picks Stroll Sock Yarn (75% superwash merino wool, 25% nylon, 1¾ oz/50g, 231 yd/211.2m): 1 (1, 1, 2) skeins in Cork (A) **①** SUPER FINE

✦ Knit Picks Stroll Glimmer Yarn (70% fine superwash merino wool, 25% nylon, 5% Stellina, 1¾ oz/50g, 231yd/211.2m): 1 skein in White (B) **①** SUPER FINE

✦ Knit Picks Stroll Glimmer Yarn (70% fine superwash merino wool, 25% nylon, 5% Stellina, 1¾ oz/50g, 231 yd/211,2m): 1 skein in Runway (C) **①** SUPER FINE

✦ Knit Picks Stroll Glimmer Yarn (70% fine superwash merino wool, 25% nylon, 5% Stellina, 1¾ oz/50g, 231 yd/211.2m): 1 skein in Foxglove (D) **①** SUPER FINE

✦ Knit Picks Stroll Glimmer Yarn (70% fine superwash merino wool, 25% nylon, 5% Stellina, 1¾ oz/50g, 231 yd/211.2m): 1 skein in Dragonscale (E) **①** SUPER FINE

✦ Set of 5 size 2 (2.74mm) double-pointed needles, or size needed to obtain gauge

✦ Stitch markers

✦ Stitch holders

✦ Tapestry needle

GAUGE

32 stitches and 40 rows = 4" (10cm) in stockinette stitch

SPECIAL INSTRUCTIONS

B = (Make bobble) Knit in front, back, front, back, and front of stitch (5 stitches). [Turn and p5; turn and k5] twice. With the left-hand needle, pass the 2nd, 3rd, 4th, and 5th stitches over the 1st stitch.

Cuff

With B, cast on 108 (121, 144, 162) stitches. Divide stitches evenly over 3 needles. Place marker and join, being careful not to twist stitches.

Knit 1 round.

Decrease Round: *K 1, k2tog; repeat from * to the last 0 (1, 0, 0) stitch, k0 (1, 0, 0)—72 (81, 96, 108) stitches.

Knit 1 round.

Decrease Round: *K1, k2tog; repeat from * around—48 (54, 64, 72) stitches.

Wrist

Change to A and work 28 (35, 35, 42) rounds in chart pattern (4 [5, 5, 6] rounds of bobbles) as follows:

For the right-hand glove: With A, k9 (11, 13, 15), work 5 stitches in chart pattern, with A, knit to end.

For the left-hand glove: With A, k34 (38, 46, 52), work 5 stitches in chart pattern, with A, knit to end.

Knit 1 round with A.

Body and Thumb Gusset

Thumb gusset setup round: K24 (27, 32, 36), pm, M1, pm, k24 (27, 32, 36)—49 (55, 65, 73) stitches.

Knit 1 round.

Increase Round: Work 24 (27, 32, 36) stitches in chart pattern, sm; with A, M1, knit to marker, M1, sm; work 24 (27, 32, 36) stitches in chart pattern—2 thumb gusset stitches increased.

Repeat Increase Round every other round until there are 13 thumb gusset stitches, then every 3rd round until there are 19 (21, 23, 25) stitches—67 (75, 87, 97) stitches total.

Place 19 (21, 23, 25) thumb gusset stitches onto a stitch holder. Distribute remaining 48 (54, 64, 72) stitches over 3 needles.

Body and Fingers

Continue working in chart pattern until 56 (70, 77, 84) rounds have been completed—8 (10, 11, 12) rounds of bobbles.

With A, knit 10 rounds.

Change to B and knit 1 round.

Increase Round: *K1, kfb; repeat from * around—72 (81, 96, 108) stitches.

Knit 1 round.

Increase Round: *K1, kfb; repeat from * to the last 0 (1, 0, 0) stitch, k0 (1, 0, 0)—108 (121, 144, 162) stitches.

Knit 1 round. Bind off.

Thumb

Distribute the 19 (21, 23, 25) thumb gusset stitches from the holder over 3 needles. Starting at the inside of the thumb with A, k9 (10, 11, 12), kfb, k9 (10, 11, 12), pick up and k2 on the inside of the thumb—22 (24, 26, 28) stitches. Place marker and join, being careful not to twist the stitches.

Knit 1 round.

Work in k1, p1 rib for ¾ (1, 1¾, 1½)" (2 [2.5, 4.5, 3.8]cm). Bind off.

Finishing

Weave in all the yarn ends.

Stitch Key

- ■ Cork (A)
- ■ Runway (C)
- ■ Foxglove (D)
- ■ Dragonscale (E)
- □ K on RS, p on WS (for all colors)
- B Make bobble = Knit in front, back, front, back, then front of same st (5 sts); [turn, p5; turn; k5] twice; do not turn, pass 2nd, 3rd, 4th, and 5th sts over first st (1 st)

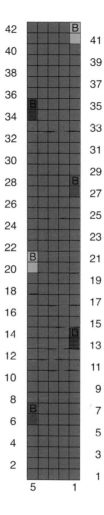

Modern Chain-Mail Hoodie

Modern knights, be they on the side of good or evil, need a comfortable
suit of armor they can wear every day, and this pullover is so soft they may
never take it off! Knit from the top down, you can try it on as you knit.
Panels of braided cables make this garter-stitch sweater fun to knit and add
just enough embellishment for a warrior princess.

DESIGNED BY MARILEE NORRIS

SKILL LEVEL

Intermediate

SIZES

Children's 4 (6, 8, 10, 12, 14,
Women's S, M, L)

FINISHED MEASUREMENTS

To fit bust/chest: 23 (25, 27, 29, 31,
33, 35, 37, 39)" (58.5 [63.5, 68.5,
74, 79, 84, 89, 94, 99]cm)

Actual bust/chest: 32 (33, 34½,
38, 40, 42, 43, 44, 45½)" (81 [84,
88, 96.5, 101.5, 106.5, 109, 112,
115.5]cm)

MATERIALS

+ Brown Sheep Lamb's Pride
  Superwash Bulky (100% wool,
  3½ oz/100g, 110 yd/100m): 8
  (9, 9, 10, 10, 11, 11, 12, 12) skeins in
  Grey Heather (A) (5) BULKY

+ Brown Sheep Lamb's Pride
  Superwash Bulky (100% wool,
  3½ oz/100g, 110 yd/100m):
  1 skein in Onyx (B) (5) BULKY

+ Size 10½ (6.5mm) 32" circular
  needle, or size needed to
  obtain gauge

+ Set of size 10½ (6.5mm)
  double-pointed needles, or size
  needed to obtain gauge

+ Stitch markers

+ Cable needle

+ Stitch holders

+ Tapestry needle

+ Size K-10½ (6.5mm) crochet
  hook

GAUGE

13 stitches and 26 rows = 4" (10cm)
in garter stitch

SPECIAL SKILLS

Cables (page 135)

Kitchener stitch (page 137)

SPECIAL INSTRUCTIONS

2/2 LC: Slip 2 stitches to cable
needle and hold in front, k2, k2
from cable needle.

2/2 RC: Slip 2 stitches to cable
needle and hold in back, k2, k2
from cable needle.

STITCH PATTERNS

Braided Cable Pattern A
Round 1: P2, k6, p2.
Round 2: P2, k2, 2/2 RC, p2.
Round 3: Repeat Round 1.
Round 4: P2, 2/2 LC, k2, p2.
Repeat Rounds 1–4 for pattern.

Braided Cable Pattern B
Row 1 (RS): P2, k2, 2/2 RC, p2.
Row 2: K2, p6, k2.
Row 3: P2, 2/2 LC, k2, p2.
Row 4: Repeat Row 2.
Repeat Rows 1–4 for pattern.

NOTE

Sweater is knit from the top
down.

Yoke

With circular needle and A, cast on 28 (34, 34, 40, 40, 40, 46, 46, 46) stitches. Do not join.

Row 1 (setup): K1, pm, k1 tbl, pm, k4 (6, 6, 8, 8, 8, 10, 10, 10), pm, k1 tbl, pm, k14 (16, 16, 18, 18, 18, 20, 20, 20), pm, k1 tbl, pm, k4 (6, 6, 8, 8, 8, 10, 10, 10), pm, k1 tbl, pm, k1.

Row 2 (WS): *Knit to marker, sm, p1 tbl, sm; repeat from * across; after last marker, knit to end.

Row 3: *Knit to 1 stitch before marker, kfb, sm, k1 tbl, sm, kfb; repeat from * across; after last marker, knit to end—8 stitches increased.

Repeat Rows 2 and 3 until there are 52 (66, 74, 80, 80, 80, 86, 86, 86) stitches.

Repeat Row 2 once more.

Next row (RS): *Kfb, knit to 1 stitch before marker, kfb, sm, k1 tbl, sm; repeat from * across; after last marker, kfb, knit to the last stitch, kfb—10 stitches increased.

Repeat last 2 rows until there are 82 (96, 104, 110, 110, 110, 116, 116, 116) stitches.

Repeat Row 2 once more.

Next row (RS): Knit to 1 stitch before marker, kfb, sm, k1 tbl, sm, *kfb, k2 (4, 5, 6, 6, 6, 8, 8, 8); pm, k10 (cable stitches for sleeve), pm, k2 (4, 5, 6, 6, 6, 8, 8, 8); kfb, sm, k1 tbl, sm**; kfb, knit to 1 stitch before marker, kfb, sm, k1 tbl, sm; repeat from * to **; at last marker, sm, kfb, knit to 1 stitch before the end, pm, k1 tbl, pm, cast on 6 (8, 8, 10, 12, 14, 16, 16, 16) stitches, pm. Do not turn—96 (112, 120, 128, 130, 132, 140, 140, 140) stitches.

Begin working in the round. Last marker designates beginning of round.

NOTE: Starting on next round, work Braided Cable Pattern A over the 10 sleeve stitches on each side only.

Next round: K1 tbl, pm, *purl to marker, sm, k1 tbl, sm, repeat from * around; after last marker, purl to end.

Next round (do not increase at the markers on each side of 10 cable stitches): K1 tbl, sm, *knit to 1 stitch before marker, kfb, sm, k1 tbl, sm, kfb; repeat from * 3 more times; knit to next marker, sm, k1 tbl, sm, knit to end.

Next round: K1 tbl, sm, *purl to marker, sm, k1 tbl, sm, repeat from * around. After the last marker, purl to end.

Repeat last 2 rounds until there are 184 (192, 200, 224, 234, 244, 252, 260, 268) stitches.

DIVIDE FOR SLEEVES AND BODY

Next round: K1 tbl, sm, *knit to 4 stitches before marker, pm, k4, remove marker, k1 tbl, remove marker; slip sleeve stitches along with the stitch markers for cable to holder; remove marker, k1 tbl, remove marker, k4, pm; repeat from *, knit to marker, sm, k1 tbl, sm, knit to end.

Body

Work in garter stitch (alternate purl and knit rounds), working marked stitches in k1 tbl as established and working Braided Cable Pattern A between markers on each side (starting on 10th round after separating sleeves and body) until body measures 11 (12, 13, 14, 14, 15, 16, 16, 16)" (28 [30.5, 33, 35.5, 35.5, 38, 41, 41, 41]cm). Bind off loosely.

Sleeves

Place held sleeve stitches on double-pointed needles. Work in garter stitch, maintaining cable pattern as established, until sleeve measures 9 (10½, 11, 12, 13, 16, 16½, 17)" (23 [26.5, 28, 30, 33, 41, 42, 43]cm). Bind off loosely.

Hood

Starting at center front, pick up and knit 46 (54, 54, 60, 60, 60, 66, 66, 66) stitches around neck opening. Knit next wrong-side row.

Row 1 (RS): K3, pm, work Row 1 of Braided Cable Pattern B, pm, knit to last 13 stitches, pm, work Row 1 of Braided Cable Pattern B, pm, k3.

Row 2: K3, *sm, work next cable row, sm**, knit to marker, repeat from * to **, k3.

Repeat Row 2 until hood measures 2¼ (2¾, 3, 3½, 3½, 3½, 4, 4, 4)" (5.5 [7, 7.5, 9, 9, 9, 10, 10, 10]cm) from back of neck, ending with a wrong-side row. Place marker in the center of the row.

***Row 3 (increase row):** K3, *sm, work next cable row, sm**, knit to 1 stitch before center marker, kfb, sm, kfb, knit to marker, repeat from * to **, k3—2 stitches increased.

Repeat Row 2 three (five, five, five, five, five, five, five, five) times, keeping in pattern as established. Repeat from *** 5 (2, 4, 4, 4, 4, 4, 4, 4) more times—58 (60, 64, 70, 70, 70, 76, 76, 76) stitches.

Work even in pattern until hood measures 10½ (11, 12, 13, 13, 13, 14, 14, 14)" (26.5 [28, 30.5, 33, 33, 33, 36, 36, 36]cm), ending with a right-side row.

Turn, work in pattern to center marker. Remove marker.

Fold the hood in half with the wrong sides together, and graft it closed using Kitchener stitch.

Finishing

Weave in ends. With crochet hook and B, work in single crochet around edge of hood and sleeve cuffs. Block.

Dragon Softie

Every little warrior needs a dragon friend like this cuddly, overstuffed guy. The toy is knit from the head down, starting inside the mouth. When picking up stitches, always pick up one row in from the edges to create a smoother look and prevent holes or gaps.

←— DESIGNED BY DAWN THOMPSON —→

SKILL LEVEL

Intermediate

SIZE

One size

FINISHED MEASUREMENTS

11" (28cm) tall

MATERIALS

✦ Red Heart Celebration (96% acrylic, 4% metallic polyester; 3½ oz/100g, 235 yd/215m): 1 skein in Lime/Silver (A)
4 MEDIUM

✦ Red Heart Celebration (96% acrylic, 4% metallic polyester; 3½ oz/100g, 235 yd/215m): 1 skein in Gold/Silver (B)
4 MEDIUM

✦ Small amount of black yarn

✦ Small amount of red yarn

✦ Size 3 (3.25mm) double-pointed needles

✦ Stitch holder

✦ Stitch markers

✦ Tapestry needle

✦ Polyester fiberfill

GAUGE

22 stitches and 36 rows = 4" in stockinette stitch

SPECIAL SKILLS

I-cord (page 136)

Embroidery stitches (page 136)

Inner Mouth

With B, cast on 7 stitches, leaving a 40" (101.5cm) tail.

Rows 1–5: Work in stockinette stitch.

Row 6 (WS): P3, p2tog, p2—6 stitches.

Rows 7–9: Work even in stockinette stitch.

Row 10: P2tog, p2, p2tog—4 stitches.

Row 11: Knit.

Bind off. The lower half of the inner mouth is complete.

For the upper half of the inner mouth, using the yarn tail, pick up and knit 7 stitches from the cast-on row and repeat Rows 1–11.

Outer Jaw

With A, pick up and knit 17 stitches around the upper half of the inner mouth.

Rows 1–3: Purl.

Row 4 (RS): K8, ssk, turn.

Row 5: P3, ssp, turn.

Row 6: K3, ssk, turn.

Repeat Rows 5 and 6 until 4 stitches remain, and place them on a holder for the top of the head. The upper jaw is now complete.

With A, pick up and knit 19 stitches around the lower half of the inner mouth, picking up the 2 extra stitches in the crease between the upper and lower halves, 1 on each side.

Rows 1–3: Purl.

Row 4 (RS): K10, ssk, turn.

Row 5: P2, ssp, turn.

Row 6: K2, ssk, turn.

Repeat Rows 5 and 6 until 7 stitches remain. Work 4 rows in stockinette stitch. Place on a holder for the neck. The lower jaw is now complete.

Top of the Head

With A, pick up and knit 4 stitches between upper and lower jaw, purl across the 4 held top-of-head stitches, pick up and knit 4 stitches between the jaws on the opposite side—12 stitches.

Rows 1 and 2: Work in stockinette stitch.

Row 3 (WS): P9, turn.

Row 4: K6, turn.

Row 5: P1, kfb, p4, kfb, p2, turn.

Row 6: K10.

Row 7: P1, kfb, p8, kfb, p2, turn.

Row 8: K14.

Row 9: P1, kfb, p12, kfb, p2—18 stitches.

Rows 10–12: Work in stockinette stitch.

Row 13: P12, turn.

Row 14: K6, turn.

Row 15: P5, p2tog, turn—17 stitches.

Row 16: K5, p2tog, turn—16 stitches.

Repeat Rows 15 and 16 until 6 stitches remain, pick up and knit 6 stitches, knit the 7 neck stitches on the holder, pick up and knit 6 stitches—25 stitches. Place marker and join into a round.

Neck

Row 1: K4, pm, k2tog, k12, k2tog, pm, k5—23 stitches.

Row 2: Knit.

Row 3: Knit to marker, sm, k2tog, knit to 2 stitches before marker, k2tog, sm, knit to end—2 stitches decreased.

Repeat these 2 rows until 17 stitches remain.

Body

NOTES: The body is now worked flat; the belly will be added into the opening later. Remove markers.

Row 1: K4, kfb, k6, kfb, knit to end—19 stitches.

Row 2: Knit.

Row 3: K4, kfb, k6, kfb, pm, k1, kfb, knit to end—22 stitches.

Row 4: K4, turn.

Row 5: Slip the first stitch purlwise, purl to end of row.

NOTE: The neck has now been split open for the belly; slip the first stitch of all body rows throughout.

Row 6 (RS): Knit to 1 stitch before marker, kfb, sm, kfb, knit to end—24 stitches.

Rows 7–9: Work in stockinette stitch.

Rows 10, 14, 18, and 22: Knit to 1 stitch before the marker, kfb, sm, kfb, knit to end.

Rows 11–13: Work in stockinette stitch.

Rows 15–17: Work in stockinette stitch.

Rows 19–21: Work in stockinette stitch.

Rows 23–25: Work in stockinette stitch.

Row 26: K2, kfb, knit to 1 stitch before marker, kfb, sm, kfb, knit to the last 2 stitches, kfb, k2.

Rows 27, 29, and 31: Purl.

Row 28: K2, kfb, knit to the last 2 stitches, kfb, k2.

Row 30: Repeat Row 26.

Working in stockinette stitch, repeat Row 10 every 4th row once, then every other row 8 times—60 stitches.

Next (decrease) row (RS): Knit to 2 stitches before marker, k2tog, sm, k1, ssk, knit to end—2 stitches decreased.

Working in stockinette stitch, repeat decrease row every other row 5 times—48 stitches. Work 4 rows even.

Next (decrease) row (RS): K1, ssk, knit to 2 stitches before marker, k2tog, sm, k1, ssk, knit to last 3 stitches, k2tog, k1—44 stitches. Place on holder.

Belly

With B and leaving a long tail for sewing, cast on 3 stitches.

Row 1 (WS): Purl.

Row 2: K1, M1, k1, M1, k1—5 stitches.

Row 3: Purl.

Row 4: K1, M1, k3, M1, k1—7 stitches.

Row 5: Knit.

Row 6: Purl.

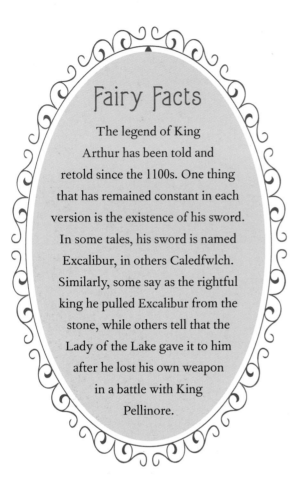

Repeat Rows 1–6, working M1 one stitch in from each end of the row every other row until there are 27 stitches.

Continue in pattern, working decrease row as follows every other row until 3 stitches remain.

Next (decrease) row (RS): K1, ssk, knit to last 3 stitches, k2tog, k1.

Purl next row. Bind off. Sew Belly into the dragon body opening.

Finishing the Body

Place the held body stitches on a needle and join in the round. Stuff the head and body before closing. Pick up 1 stitch from the base of the Belly—45 stitches.

Round 1: Knit.

Round 2: K3, k2tog to end—36 stitches.

Round 3: Knit.

Round 4: K2, k2tog to end—27 stitches.

Round 5: Knit.

Round 6: K1, k2tog to end—18 stitches.

Round 7: Knit.

Round 8: K2tog to end—9 stitches.

Draw yarn through remaining stitches and fasten off.

Back Legs (make 2)

With A, cast on 6 stitches.

Round 1 (work as I-cord): [Kfb] 6 times—12 stitches.

Round 2: (K1, kfb) to end—18 stitches.

Round 3: (K2, kfb) to end—24 stitches.

Round 3: (K3, kfb) to end—30 stitches.

Round 4: (K4, kfb) to end—36 stitches.

Round 5: Knit.

Round 6: (K5, kfb) to end—42 stitches.

Knit 10 rounds.

Round 17: (K12, k2tog) to end—39 stitches.

Round 18: Knit.

Round 19: (K11, k2tog) to end—36 stitches.

Knit 3 rounds.

Round 23: (K10, k2tog) to end—33 stitches.

Knit 3 rounds.

Round 27: (K9, k2tog) to end—30 stitches.

Knit 3 rounds.

Bind off. Stuff and sew the Back Legs to the bottom of the body, with legs placed 3 stitches away from the Belly.

Claws (make 4)

With B, cast on 2 stitches.

Work in I-cord for 18 rounds.

Bind off.

Draw I-cord through the Back Legs so that each I-cord creates 2 Claws placed 6 stitches apart.

Forelegs (make 2)

With A, cast on 6 stitches.

Round 1 (work as I-cord): [Kfb] 6 times—12 stitches.

Round 2: Knit.

Round 3: (K1, kfb) to end—18 stitches.

Round 4: Knit.

Round 5: (K2, kfb) to end—24 stitches.

Knit 14 rounds.

Round 20: (K10, k2tog) to end—22 stitches.

Knit 2 rounds.

Knit 23: (K9, k2tog) to end—20 stitches.

Knit 2 rounds.

Bind off. Stuff and sew Forelegs to the sides of the body, with Forelegs placed 3 stitches away from the Belly.

Tail

With A, cast on 30 stitches and join in the round.

Knit 10 rounds.

Round 11: (K8, k2tog) to end—27 stitches.

Round 12: (K7, k2tog) to end—24 stitches.

Knit 2 rounds.

Round 15: (K6, k2tog) to end—21 stitches.

Round 16: Knit.

Round 17: (K5, k2tog) to end—18 stitches.

Round 18: (K4, k2tog) to end—15 stitches.

Round 19: (K3, k2tog) to end—12 stitches.

Round 20: (K2, k2tog) to end—9 stitches.

Round 21: (K2, k2tog) to end—6 stitches.

Draw the yarn through the remaining stitches and fasten off. Stuff and sew the Tail to the back of the body.

Wings (make 2 pairs)

With B, cast on 12 stitches.

Work in reverse stockinette stitch for 5 rows.

Next (increase) row (WS): K1, kfb, knit to last 2 stitches, kfb, k1—14 stitches.

Create the other side of the wing, reversing shaping. Place two sides of one Wing with right (purl) sides together and seam, leaving an opening. Turn Wing inside out, lightly stuff, and close opening. Repeat for second Wing. Sew completed Wings to the back of the body, behind the Forelegs.

Spikes

With B and starting at the middle of the top of the head, pick up and knit 1 stitch every 2nd row to the neck, then pick up in every 3rd row along the neck, and then in every other row to the top of the wings.

Row 1: Knit.

Row 2: (Knit into the front, back, and front of the same stitch, k3) to end.

Row 3: Bind off first 4 stitches, *k3 in 1, k1, k3 in 1, k4; repeat from * to last 2 stitches, k2tog. Bind off loosely.

Nostrils

With A, cast on 2 stitches.

Work I-cord for 22 rounds.

Weave I-cord in and out of the top jaw, so that each Nostril spans 3 stitches, placed 2 stitches apart.

Finishing

Cut a strand of red yarn 2" (5cm) long.

Tie a knot ¼" (6mm) from the end of the strand. Weave the other end into the mouth.

Embroider eyes with satin stitch (page 136) using B and black.

Continue working in reverse stockinette stitch, repeating increase row on next 3 wrong-side rows—20 stitches.

Work 8 rows in reverse stockinette stitch.

Next (decrease) row (WS): K1, k2tog, knit to end—1 stitch decreased—19 stitches.

Work in reverse stockinette, repeating decrease row 6 more times—13 stitches.

Decrease 1 stitch on both right and wrong sides of work 4 times—9 stitches.

Bind off.

Queen of Hearts Beret

Off with their heads! When you're in a furious mood, wear
this gorgeous Fair Isle beret to remind everyone who's the boss.
The color palette was chosen from the deck of cards that
Alice stumbles across during her adventures in Wonderland, and this
pattern makes for a fun introduction to stranded knitting.

←— DESIGNED BY TANIS GRAY —→

SKILL LEVEL

Intermediate

SIZE

One size

FINISHED MEASUREMENTS

21" (53.5cm) circumference

MATERIALS

✦ Tanis Fiber Arts Green Label
Aran Weight (100% superwash
merino wool, 4 oz/113g,
205 yd/187m), 1 skein in
Charcoal (A) (4) MEDIUM

✦ Tanis Fiber Arts Green Label
Aran Weight (100% superwash
merino wool, 4 oz/113g,
205 yd/187m), 1 skein in Poppy
(B) (4) MEDIUM

✦ Tanis Fiber Arts Green Label
Aran Weight (100% superwash
merino wool, 4 oz/113g,
205 yd/187m), 1 skein in Dove
(C) (4) MEDIUM

✦ Tanis Fiber Arts Green Label
Aran Weight (100% superwash
merino wool, 4 oz/113g,
205 yd/187m), 1 skein in Natural
(D) (4) MEDIUM

✦ Size 6 (4mm) 16" circular needle,
or size needed to obtain gauge

✦ Size 7 (4.5mm) 16" circular
needle, or size needed to
obtain gauge

✦ Set of 5 size 7 (4.5mm) double-
pointed needles, or size
needed to obtain gauge

✦ Stitch markers

✦ Tapestry needle

GAUGE

18 stitches and 29 rows = 4"
(10cm) in rib pattern using smaller
needles

20 stitches and 22 rows = 4"
(10cm) in Fair Isle pattern using
larger needles

SPECIAL SKILLS

Stranded knitting (page 139)

STITCH PATTERNS

See charts (page 121)

NOTE

Carry all colors inside the work;
do not break yarns until the end.

Beret

With smaller needle and A, cast on 96 stitches. Place marker and join, being careful not to twist the stitches. Work Rounds 1–10 of Rib chart. Change to larger circular needle. Work Rounds 1–12 of Brim chart.

Round 22: *K2, M1; repeat from * around—144 stitches. Place a marker every 18 stitches.

Work Rounds 1–23 of Crown chart, changing to double-pointed needles when needed.

Next round: With B, *k2tog; repeat from * around—8 stitches.

Break yarn, draw through remaining stitches, pull tight, and secure.

Finishing

Weave in ends. Block well, using a bowl to set the shape.

Stitch Key

■	Charcoal (A)	⊡	Purl
■	Poppy (B)	◪	K2tog
■	Dove (C)	◩	Ssk
□	Natural (D)	M	Make 1
□	Knit	■	No stitch
		□	Repeat

Rib

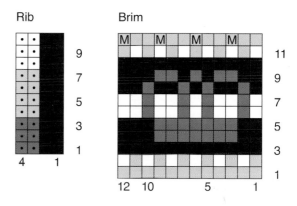

Brim

Crown

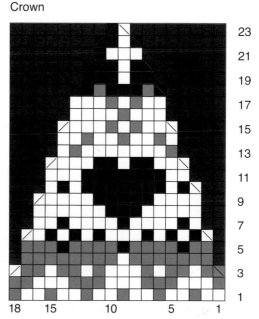

Rumpelstiltskin Infinity Scarf

Inspired by the constant shimmer of Rumpelstiltskin's skin in *Once Upon a Time*, this cowl mimics his talent for seamlessly twisting and manipulating situations until no one is sure what his motives might be. Knit in an easy slanted pattern, this scarf knits up quickly in a bulky-weight yarn that looks exactly like straw that has been spun into gold.

←— DESIGNED BY JOAN OF DARK (A.K.A. TONI CARR) —→

SKILL LEVEL

Easy

SIZE

One size

FINISHED MEASUREMENTS

50" (127cm) circumference x 5¾" (14.5cm) wide

MATERIALS

✦ Bergere de France Galaxie (80% acrylic, 18% wool, 2% polyester, 1¾ oz/50g, 38 yd/35m): 4 skeins in Centaure (5) BULKY

✦ 2 size 10 (6mm) 16" circular needles, or size needed to obtain gauge

✦ Tapestry needle

GAUGE

15 stitches and 19 rows = 4" (10cm) in stockinette stitch

SPECIAL SKILLS

Provisional cast-on (page 138)

Kitchener stitch (page 137)

Scarf

NOTE: If desired, cast on using scrap yarn instead of the spare circular, though a spare needle will still be required to work the Kitchener stitch seam.

Cast on 16 stitches with a provisional cast-on. Using the second needle (leave the needle used for cast-on as a stitch holder for now), work as follows:

K1, *yo, k2tog; repeat from * to the last stitch, k1.

Repeat until the piece measures 50" (127cm). Do not bind off.

Finishing

Without binding off, turn the end of the scarf once to create the twisted infinity loop, then join the two ends using the Kitchener stitch. Weave in the ends.

An Apple a Day

In *Once Upon a Time*, the evil queen from Snow White
is Regina Mills, the mayor of Storybrooke known for her beloved
Honey Crisp apple tree (and poisoned turnovers). This cheerful
pot holder makes the perfect gift when paired with a basket of sinful
treats. No one will ever suspect your deliciously evil plans.

← DESIGNED BY ABIGAIL HORSFALL →

SKILL LEVEL

Intermediate

SIZE

One Size

FINISHED MEASUREMENTS

8" x 8" (20.5cm x 20.5cm)

MATERIALS

- Knit Picks Swish Worsted
  (100% merino wool,
  1¾ oz/100g, 110 yd/100.5m):
  1 ball in Hollyberry (A)
  4 MEDIUM

- Knit Picks Swish Worsted
  (100% merino wool,
  1¾ oz/100g, 110 yd/100.5m):
  1 ball in Serrano (B) **4 MEDIUM**

- Knit Picks Swish Worsted
  (100% merino wool,
  1¾ oz/100g, 110 yd/100.5m):
  1 ball in Dublin (C) **4 MEDIUM**

- Size 5 (3.75mm) straight
  needles, or size needed to
  obtain gauge

- Set of 2 US 5 (3.75mm) double-
  pointed needles

- Stitch holder

- Tapestry needle

GAUGE

16 stitches and 32 rows = 4" (10cm)
in garter stitch

SPECIAL SKILLS

I-cord (page 136)

NOTE

This pattern is worked at a
worsted gauge using worsted-
weight yarn held doubled to
ensure a sturdy, thick fabric that
will insulate from heat for use
as a pot holder. Please choose
carefully if yarn substitutions are
made. Do not use acrylic yarn,
which may melt, unless the pot
holder is intended purely for
decoration.

Pot Holder

With one strand each of A and B held together, cast on 15 stitches.

Row 1 (WS): Knit.

Row 2: Kfb, knit to the last 2 stitches, kfb, k1—2 stitches increased.

Rows 3–16: Repeat Rows 1 and 2—31 stitches after Row 16.

Rows 17–19: Knit.

Row 20: Repeat Row 2—33 stitches.

Rows 21–24: Repeat Rows 17–20—35 stitches.

Rows 25–41: Knit.

Row 42: K1, ssk, knit to the last 3 stitches, k2tog, k1—2 stitches decreased.

Rows 43–45: Knit.

Row 46: Repeat Row 42—31 stitches.

Rows 47–54: Repeat Rows 43–46—27 stitches after Row 54.

Row 55: Knit.

Row 56: K1, ssk, k8, k2tog, bind off 1 stitch, ssk, k8, k2tog, k1—22 stitches.

There are now two sets of live stitches that will be worked separately. Continue working on the second set of 11 stitches, setting aside the first set on a stitch holder for now.

Row 57 (WS): K1, ssk, k5, k2tog, k1—9 stitches.

Row 58: K1, ssk, k3, k2tog, k1—7 stitches.

Row 59: K1, ssk, k1, k2tog, k1—5 stitches.

Bind off 5 stitches and break yarn.

Return to the first set of 11 stitches and join yarn with the wrong side facing.

Repeat Rows 57–59.

Bind off 5 stitches and break yarn.

Stem

With double-pointed needles and 2 strands of C held together, pick up 3 stitches at the center of the top of the apple, between the two top pieces, and work in I-cord for 1½" (3.8cm).

Leaf

With 2 strands of C held together, cast on 2 stitches.

Row 1 (RS): Kfb, k1—3 stitches.

Row 2 and every WS row: Purl.

Row 3: Kfb, kfb, k1—5 stitches.

Row 5: Kfb, k1, kfb, k1, kfb—8 stitches.

Rows 7, 9, and 11: K1, p2, k2, p2, k1.

Row 13: Ssk, k1, k2tog, k1, k2tog—5 stitches.

Row 15: Ssk, k1, k2tog—3 stitches.

Row 17: Sk2p—1 stitch.

Break yarn and pull it through the remaining stitch. Sew the leaf to the apple using the cast-on tail, with one point touching the stem.

Weave in all ends.

Elsa Snow Vest

Perfect for driving a sled through drifts of snow, this body-conscious vest is designed to fit without any ease. A stand-up, short-row collar and sparkling crystal accents at the waistline add regal drama, while a built-in garter selvedge edge makes seaming a breeze and lends a sporty, neat appearance to the side seams and armhole edges.

← DESIGNED BY CIRILIA ROSE →

SKILL LEVEL

Intermediate

SIZES

XS (S, M, L, XL)

FINISHED MEASUREMENTS

Bust: 33½ (38, 40, 43½, 50)" (85 [96.5, 101.5, 110.5, 127]cm)

Length: 25¾ (26¼, 27¼, 27¾, 29¼)" (65.5 [66.5, 69, 70.5, 74.5 cm)

MATERIALS

✦ Schoppel Wolle XL (100% merino wool, 3½ oz/100g, 72 yd/66m): 8 (9, 10, 11, 12) skeins in 0980 White Chocolate (6) SUPER BULKY

✦ Size 13 (9mm) 24" circular needle, or size needed to obtain gauge

✦ Cable needle

✦ Stitch holders or scrap yarn

✦ Tapestry needle

✦ 22 (22, 23, 24, 25)" (56 [56, 58.5, 61, 63.5]cm) separating metallic zipper

✦ Sewing needle and matching thread

✦ 16 (20, 21, 24, 25) crystal accents (shown are Create Your Style Swarovski Elements Tanzanite Square Sliders)

GAUGE

11 stitches and 13 rows = 4" (10cm) in Wide Rib pattern

SPECIAL INSTRUCTIONS

RC: Slip 1 stitch to cable needle and hold in back, k1, k1 from cable needle.

LC: Slip 1 stitch to cable needle and hold in front, k1, k1 from cable needle.

RPC: Slip 1 stitch to cable needle and hold in back, p1, k1 from cable needle.

LPC: Slip 1 stitch to cable needle and hold in front, p1, k1 from cable needle.

SPECIAL STITCHES

Garter Selvedge Edge (worked over first and last 2 sts of each row)
Row 1 (RS): sl 1 st kwise, k1, proceed with pattern to last 2 sts, k2.
Row 2: rep Row 1.

Wide Rib (multiple of 5)
Row 1 (RS): *P2, k1, p2; repeat from * to end.
Row 2: *K2, p1, k2; repeat from * to end.

Narrow Rib (multiple of 3)
Row 1 (RS): *P1, k1, p1; repeat from * to end.
Row 2: *K1, p1, k1; repeat from * to end.

Back

Cast on 44 (54, 59, 64, 69) stitches.

Row 1 (RS): Sl 1, k1, p2, *k1, p4; repeat from * to the last 5 stitches, k1, p2, k2.

Row 2: Sl 1, k3, *p1, k4; repeat from * to end.

Repeat these 2 rows for Wide Rib pattern until piece measures 8" (20.5cm) from the cast-on edge, ending with a wrong-side row.

WAIST SHAPING

Row 1: Sl 1, k1, *RC, k1, LC; repeat from * to the last 2 stitches, k2.

Rows 2 and 4: Sl 1, k1, purl to the last 2 stitches, k2.

Row 3: Sl 1, knit to end.

Row 5: Sl 1, k1, *LPC, k1, RPC; repeat from * to the last 2 stitches, k2.

Row 6: Sl 1, *k2, p3; repeat from * to the last 3 stitches, k3.

Row 7: Sl 1, k1, *p1, s2kp, p1; repeat from * to the last 3 stitches, p1, k2—28 (34, 37, 40, 43) stitches.

Row 8: Sl 1, k2, *p1, k2; repeat from * to the last stitch, k1.

Continue in Narrow Rib as established for 1" (2.5cm), ending with a wrong-side row.

BODICE

Increase Row (RS): Sl 1, k1, M1R, p1, *k1, p2; repeat from * to the last 4 stitches, k1, p1, M1L, k2—2 stitches increased.

Repeat Increase Row every right-side row 8 (8, 8, 9, 12) times more, incorporating new stitches into the Narrow Rib pattern—46 (52, 55, 60, 69) stitches.

Sizes L (XL) only: Increase 1 stitch at the beginning OR the end of the last wrong-side row—61 (70) stitches.

Continue in Narrow Rib as established until body measures 17 (17½, 17½, 18, 18½)" (43 [44.5, 44.5, 45.5, 47]cm), ending with a wrong-side row.

SHAPE ARMHOLES

Bind off 2 (2, 2, 3, 4) stitches at the beginning of the next 6 rows—34 (40, 43, 43, 46) stitches.

Reestablish the 2 selvedge stitches at each end and continue to work in rib as established until armholes measure 7 (7, 8, 8, 9)" (18 [18, 20.5, 20.5, 23]cm).

SHAPE SHOULDERS

Bind off 2 (3, 3, 3, 3) stitches at the beginning of the next 6 rows. Slip the remaining 22 (22, 25, 25, 25) stitches to a holder or scrap yarn—6 (9, 9, 9, 9) stitches each shoulder.

Right Front

Cast on 24 (29, 29, 34, 34) stitches. Work same as Back through Row 8 of Waist Shaping—16 (19, 19, 22, 22) stitches.

Continue in Narrow Rib as established for 1" (2.5cm), ending with a wrong-side row.

BODICE

Increase Row (RS): Work in pattern as established to the last 2 stitches, M1L, k2—1 stitch increased.

Repeat Increase Row every right-side row 8 (8, 8, 10, 13) times more, incorporating new stitches into Narrow Rib pattern—25 (28, 28, 33, 36) stitches.

Continue in rib as established until piece measures 17 (17½, 17½, 18, 18½)" (43 [44.5, 44.5, 45.5, 47] cm), ending with a right-side row.

SHAPE ARMHOLE

Bind off 2 (2, 2, 3, 4) stitches at the beginning of the next 3 wrong-side rows—19 (22, 22, 24, 24) stitches.

Reestablish the 2 selvedge edges and continue to work in rib as established until armhole measures 5 (6, 7, 7, 8)" (12.5 [15, 18, 18, 20.5)cm], ending with a wrong-side row.

SHAPE NECK AND SHOULDER

Decrease Row (RS): Sl 1, k1, p1, ssk, continue in pattern as established to end.

Repeat Decrease Row every 4th row 2 (1, 0, 1, 1) time(s) more—16 (20, 21, 22, 22) stitches.

AT THE SAME TIME, when armhole measures 7 (7, 8, 8, 9)" (18 [18, 20.5, 20.5, 23]cm), ending with a right-side row, bind off 2 (3, 3, 3, 3) stitches at the beginning of the next 3 wrong-side rows. Slip the remaining 10 (11, 12, 13, 13) stitches to a holder or scrap yarn.

Left Front

Cast on 24 (29, 29, 34, 34) stitches. Work same as Back through Row 8 of Waist Shaping—16 (19, 19, 22, 22) stitches.

Continue in rib as established for 1" (2.5cm), ending with a wrong-side row.

BODICE

Increase Row (RS): Sl 1, k1, M1R, work in pattern as established to end—1 stitch increased.

Repeat Increase Row every right-side row 8 (8, 8, 10, 13) times more, incorporating new stitches into rib pattern—25 (28, 28, 33, 36) stitches.

Continue in rib as established until piece measures 17 (17½, 17½, 18, 18½)" (43 [44.5, 44.5, 45.5, 47] cm), ending with a wrong-side row.

SHAPE ARMHOLE

Bind off 2 (2, 2, 3, 4) stitches at the beginning of the next 3 right-side rows—19 (22, 22, 24, 24) stitches.

Reestablish the 2 selvedge edges and continue to work in rib as established until armhole measures 5 (6, 7, 7, 8)" (12.5 [15, 18, 18, 20.5])cm, ending with a wrong-side row.

SHAPE NECK AND SHOULDER

Decrease Row (RS): Work in pattern as established to the last 5 stitches, k2tog, p1, k2.

Repeat Decrease Row every 4th row 2 (1, 0, 1, 1) time(s) more—16 (20, 21, 22, 22) stitches.

AT THE SAME TIME, when armhole measures 7 (7, 8, 8, 9)" (18 [18, 20.5, 20.5, 23]cm), ending with a wrong-side row, bind off 2 (3, 3, 3, 3) stitches at the beginning of the next 3 right-side rows. Slip the remaining 10 (11, 12, 13, 13) stitches to a holder or scrap yarn.

Finishing

Sew shoulder seams.

NECK BAND

Place 11 (11, 12, 13, 13) Right Front stitches, 22 (22, 25, 25, 25) Back Neck stitches, and 11 (11, 12, 13, 13) Left Front stitches onto the needle—44 (44, 49, 51, 51) stitches.

Starting with a wrong-side row, knit 10 rows. Bind off knitwise on the next wrong-side row.

Gently steam-block all the pieces. Sew side seams. Insert zipper. With the zipper closed, pin both sides in place, being sure not to stretch the front edges. With a contrasting-colored thread, baste each side to the zipper, then unzip. With the matching thread, and using backstitch, sew the zipper in place, tucking the top ends of the zipper between the zipper and the garment. If necessary, whipstitch the edges of the zipper to the garment.

Sew a crystal accent to the center of each waist motif.

Knitting Abbreviations

B—make bobble

CC—contrast color

DPN—double-pointed needle

K—knit

K2tog—knit 2 together to decrease

Kfb—knit in front and back to increase

M1—make 1 stitch to increase

M1L—make 1 stitch to increase on left

M1R—make 1 stitch to increase on right

MC—main color

P—purl

P2tog—purl 2 together to decrease

Pfb—purl in front and back to increase

Pm—place marker

Psso—pass stitch over to decrease

Skp—slip, knit, pass stitch over to decrease

Sl—slip

Sm—slip marker

S2kp—slip 2, knit 1, pass slipped stitches over to decrease

Sk2p—slip 1, knit 2 together, pass slipped stitches over to decrease

Ssk—slip, slip, knit to decrease

Ssp—slip, slip, purl to decrease

Tbl—through the back loop

Wyib—with yarn in back

Wyif—with yarn in front

Yo—yarn over

Skill Levels

EASY

Uses basic stitches, repetitive stitch patterns, and simple pattern changes. Involves simple shaping and finishing.

INTERMEDIATE

Uses a variety of stitches and techniques, such as basic cables and lace, simple intarsia, double-pointed needles, and knitting in the round, with midlevel shaping and finishing.

EXPERIENCED

Involves intricate stitch patterns, techniques, and dimension, such as nonrepeating patterns, multicolored techniques, fine threads, detailed shaping, and refined finishing.

Standard Yarn Weight System

Yarn Weight Category and Symbol	● 0 LACE	● 1 SUPER FINE	● 2 FINE	● 3 LIGHT	● 4 MEDIUM	● 5 BULKY	● 6 SUPER BULKY
Types of Yarn	Fingering, 10-count crochet thread	Sock, fingering, baby	Sport, baby	DK, light worsted	Worsted, afghan, aran	Chunky, craft, rug	Bulky, roving
Knit Gauge Range (in Stockinette Stitch to 4 inches)	33–40 sts	27–32 sts	23–26 sts	21–24 sts	16–20 sts	12–15 sts	6–11 sts
Recommended Needle Sizes (US/ Metric Sizes)	00–1/1.5–2.25mm	1–3/2.25–3.25mm	3–5/3.25–3.75mm	5–7/3.75–4.5mm	7–9/4.5–5.5mm	9–11/5.5–8mm	11 and larger/8mm and larger

Adapted from the Standard Yarn Weight System of the Craft Yarn Council of America (www.yarnstandards.com)

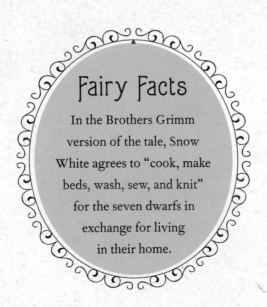

Fairy Facts

In the Brothers Grimm version of the tale, Snow White agrees to "cook, make beds, wash, sew, and knit" for the seven dwarfs in exchange for living in their home.

Special Skills

Left Cable

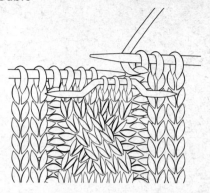

3-NEEDLE BIND-OFF

Use this technique to bind off two pieces, creating a seam between them, such as the shoulder seams in a sweater.

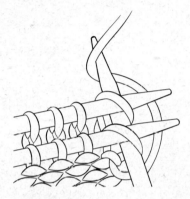

Hold the two knit pieces with right sides facing each other (unless the pattern indicates otherwise). With a third needle, knit into the first stitch on each needle, knitting these two stitches together. Repeat with the second stitch on both needles, then pull the first stitch over the second. Continue across the row until all stitches are bound off.

CABLES

Cables are twisted stitches that make your knitted piece appear to have been braided. To make a cable, place the first half of the stitches in the cable pattern on a cable needle, knit the second half, then knit the stitches on the cable needle. The stitches will magically twist! Refer to the pattern to determine how many stitches to place on the separate needle, and whether to hold them to the front (left-leaning) or the back (right-leaning).

1. Slip the next few stitches onto the cable needle. In this example, 3 stitches are slipped, but refer to your specific pattern. Hold the cable needle in front of the work.

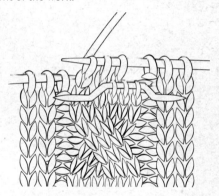

2. Knit the next group of stitches. Again, refer to your pattern.

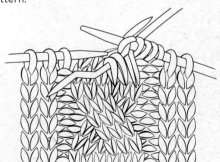

3. Knit the stitches from the cable needle.

DUPLICATE STITCH

This stitch is added on top of an already knitted piece in stockinette stitch.

Thread a tapestry needle with the desired color. Just below the knit stitch you want to cover, draw the needle from the back through to the front. Bring the thread over the right-hand leg of the stitch, down into the fabric at the top of the stitch, and up again at the bottom. Cover the left-hand leg in the same way. Repeat, following the color chart for your pattern.

EMBROIDERY STITCHES

Using embroidery floss, use the following diagrams to create two kinds of embroidered stitches on top of your knitting.

Satin Stitch

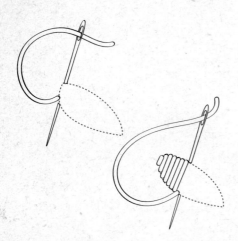

French Knots

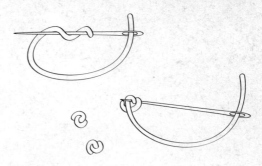

I-CORD

Create a knitted tube using two double-pointed needles.

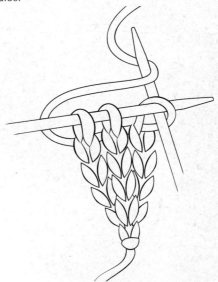

Cast on the number of stitches specified in the pattern. Knit one row. Slide the stitches to the other end of the needle, keeping the double-pointed needle in the same hand. Pull the working yarn tight across the back and knit the first stitch. Repeat for as many rows as necessary for the desired length, gently pulling on the I-cord as it forms.

KITCHENER STITCH

Use Kitchener stitch to seamlessly graft two live ends of knitting. These instructions are for grafting stockinette stitch.

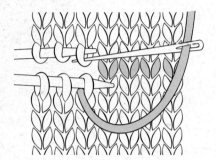

Thread a tapestry needle with a strand of yarn three to four times the length of the edge being grafted. Hold the needles with an equal number of live stitches parallel to each other with the needle tips pointing in the same direction and the right (knit) sides facing up. Insert the tapestry needle purlwise into the first stitch of the front knitting needle, draw the yarn through, but do not drop the stitch from the needle. Insert the tapestry needle knitwise into the first stitch on the back knitting needle. Draw the yarn through. Do not drop the stitch from the knitting needle. *Insert the tapestry needle knitwise into the first stitch on the front needle, drop the stitch from the needle. Insert the tapestry needle purlwise into the next stitch on the front needle. Draw the yarn through. Do not drop the stitch from the knitting needle. Insert the needle purlwise into the first stitch on the back needle. Drop the stitch from the knitting needle. Insert the tapestry needle knitwise into the next stitch on the back needle, and draw the yarn through without dropping the stitch.* Repeat from * to * until all live stitches have been grafted.

KNITTED CAST-ON

Make a slip knot and insert the right-hand needle into the loop on the left-hand needle.

Start to make a knit stitch, only after sliding the stitch off the left needle onto the right, turn the right needle and slip the finished stitch back onto the left-hand needle, pulling the yarn tight.

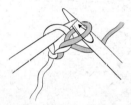

There will be two stitches on the left-hand needle. Repeat for the desired number of stitches.

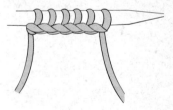

MAGIC LOOP

Magic Loop is a method of knitting small circumferences in the round using one long circular needle.

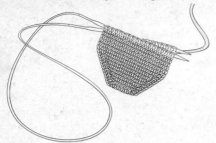

Transfer your stitches to a long circular needle when indicated in the pattern and divide the stitches with half on the front needle and half on the back needle.

Pull the cable of the circular needle so that the back stitches now rest on the cable. Use the free needle to begin knitting in the round. Keep transferring the stitches between the cable and needle as necessary.

PROVISIONAL CAST-ON

A provisional, or crocheted, cast-on allows the bottom stitches of your fabric to be grafted seamlessly using Kitchener stitch (page 137).

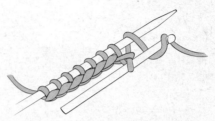

Using a crochet hook and strand of scrap yarn, wrap the yarn over the needle and draw the yarn through the hook to secure the cast on stitch to the needle.

Repeat as necessary until you have cast on as many stitches as the pattern indicates.

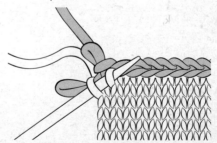

To graft the cast-on stitches to the live stitches, pick up the live stitches with an empty needle and pull out the scrap yarn that you used to cast on.

SHORT ROWS

Short rows are used to shape a piece of knitting. The method used to do this is called wrap and turn. Short rows are only partially worked before turning. Before turning a short row, you will wrap the next stitch to avoid create holes at the turns. When working the next row, you will pick up the wrap with the stitch and thus hide the wrap.

Wrap and Turn (W + T)

1. Knit to the specified stitch and slip this stitch onto the right-hand needle. Bring the yarn from the back to the front to "wrap" the stitch.

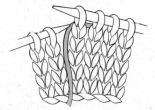

2. Slip the same stitch back to the left-hand needle.

3. Turn the work, bringing the yarn to the front (for knitting) or back (for purling) to complete the wrap. Finish working the row.

UNWRAPPING KNIT STITCHES

Insert the needle under the wrap from the bottom to top, front to back, then knitwise into the stitch. Knit the wrap and stitch together.

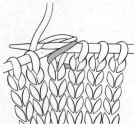

UNWRAPPING PURL STITCHES

Insert the needle into the wrap from the bottom to top, back to front, then purlwise into the stitch itself. Purl the wrap and stitch together.

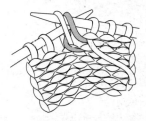

STRANDED KNITTING

When knitting with two colors at the same time, carry both yarns together but keep the yarn not in use along the back of the knitting. Keep this yarn on the back fairly loose; if it's pulled too tight it will distort the design.

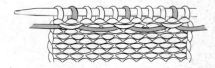

As you knit, wrap the yarn not being used around the working yarn every few stitches to keep it secure.

Contributing Designers

Joan of Dark sometimes goes by the name Toni Carr, but not very often. Formerly a roller girl, she now owns Strange Brew Coffee in Indiana and surrounds herself with a husband, a dog, cats, a parrot, a llama, and a mini horse. When she's not skating, knitting, or making coffee, she tries to learn aerial silks without breaking too many bones. She has two books out, *Knockdown Knits* and *Knits for Nerds*. You can follow her adventures at www.joanofdark.com.

Cassie Castillo is a knitwear designer and military spouse. In addition to knitting, she enjoys spinning, weaving, crocheting, sewing, and dyeing. Her faithful companion Che is guardian of the yarn. You can visit her website at www.azaleaandrosebudknits.com.

Tanis Gray lives in Alexandria, Virginia, with her green mechanical-engineer husband, toddler son, and lazy pug. The author of *Knit Local* and *Capitol Knits*, when she's not knitting, Tanis is out taking photographs, cycling, or chasing her son. Follow her at www.tanisknits.com.

Laura Hohman is a biologist, roller-derby girl, and knitter. She lives in the rolling hills of southern Indiana with a husband, one dog, three cats, three bats, and five ducks. You can find her online at www.battyknits.blogspot.com. In real life you can frequently find her at local sci-fantasy conventions, microbreweries, or derby bouts.

Abigail Horsfall lives in the Seattle area with her husband and two clever cats. By day she convinces sixth graders that fractions are their friends. By night she knits and designs. Abigail enjoys knitting, traveling, skiing, and reading—and always wishes for a way to do them all simultaneously! She blogs, with friends, at www.taatdesigns.wordpress.com.

Marilee Norris lives happily ever after in the beautiful Pacific Northwest where her handsome husband and two wonderful children keep her very busy. You can find more of her work published in *Vampire Knits* and *Knits for Nerds*.

Trisha Paetsch is a fairy-tale princess who lives in the Great White North with Prince Charming and two petite princes. She takes quite a bit of time out from sweeping her castle and singing to birds to create wonderful things with yarn. Her other work is heralded on Ravelry and at www.taatdesigns. wordpress.com.

Rilana Riley-Munson, or PDX Princess, is a part-time knitwear designer who resides in the lovely city of Portland, Oregon. When not knitting, she likes spending time with her family, cooking, reading, and wrangling her two cats. She can be found on Ravelry as "rilana," or visit her blog at www.pdx-princess.blogspot.com.

Cirilia Rose knits and designs in the Northwest and has worked for WEBS, Berroco, and Skacel. She is inspired by all things media related. Visit Cirilia at www.bricoleurknits.com.

Dawn Thompson is an elementary school teacher in Grande Prairie, Alberta. She's married, with a nine-year-old son and newborn daughter, and has a crazy shichi (shih tzu–Chihuahua cross) named Honeybun. She likes experimenting with improvisational knitting and exploring on road trips during summer break.

Index

Page references in *italic* refer to illustrations.

About the Author

GENEVIEVE MILLER is a California girl who's been knitting since she was a child. She is married to her own Prince Charming and is the mother of one prince and two princesses. After teaching kindergarten, fourth grade, and the dramatic arts for eight years, Genevieve took time off to be a stay-at-home mom. She is passing on her love of knitting to her children, as well as teaching students at her children's school. Genevieve is the author of *Vampire Knits,* and her designs can also be found in *Knits for Nerds.* You can find her these days knitting, hanging out with her family, or teaching herself photography. Follow her at www.genevieveknits.wordpress.com and @vampireknits on Twitter.